You're a leader, now what?

The proven path to high performance leadership

Mick Spiers

ISBN: 978-981-18-2456-2

This book is dedicated to my beautiful and supportive wife, Sei, and my two sons, Henry and Thomas. May the lessons in this book serve you well as you grow to be future leaders of a new generation.

I would also like to thank the many leaders I have had in my career that have helped me to become the leader I am today.

Contents

Foreword

Who is this book for?

This book is for anyone promoted into a leadership role. The transition to leadership may be far more challenging than you've expected. You may have been an outstanding individual contributor and now you are finding leadership to be a whole new ball game.

Leaders come in all shapes and sizes. The book is written around leaders in industry or business. However, the lessons within are applicable to people working in other sectors. You may be in not-for-profit organizations, charities, community organizations, churches and religious groups, government departments, schools, universities, and almost any team situation. It is also a very useful reference for long-term leaders. Leaders looking to sharpen the saw. Leaders looking to mentor the next generation of leaders.

The Proven Path to High Performance Leadership

Do you want to become a high-performance leader that inspires your team with vision, purpose, and impact? Are you seeking the skills and knowledge you need to transition into leadership roles? Are you finding leadership to be more challenging than you anticipated? Do you want to continually improve your leadership? Have you found that your career has reached a limit? Are you finding it hard to break through to the next level of leadership?

This book will help you progress and become the leader that you want to be and achieve the success you deserve.

About the Author

I am blessed to have enjoyed a very successful and diverse career. I have led global businesses with revenues of up to $300 million USD. I have sat on the executive of $1 billion multinational companies.

I have held a wide variety of roles including Engineering, Quality Management, Trainer, Consultant, Process Improvement, Bid Management, Project Management, Sales, Marketing, Strategy, and General Management. This diversity of roles has strongly contributed to my learnings as a leader.

The common thread throughout my career has been a focus on leadership. It has *not* been smooth sailing every step of the way. I have had my fair share of missteps and failures, some of which are documented in this book. However, I maintained a learning mindset throughout. Learning from successes and failures alike.

My leadership journey led to a deep study of psychology to understand human behavior and to qualifications as a certified professional coach in Transformative Coaching.

I continue to study every single day, and I am always learning from people and experiences around me.

The Leadership Project Movement

I started The Leadership Project movement with the vision to inspire all leaders to challenge the status quo. To get people to stop, reflect, and rethink what it means to be a leader. Our mission is to empower leaders with the tools and skills they need to create amazing teams and workspaces— workspaces where everyone finds purpose and meaning in what they do, where people feel their voices are heard and their opinions valued, where everyone feels that they individually and collectively matter.

The world is facing an unprecedented leadership crisis. Research from Gallup (State of the Global Workplace: 2021 Report)[1] shows that only 20 percent of people in the world are engaged at work and truly love their job and like their boss. The same report shows that 43% of workers experience <u>daily</u> stress in the workplace. People are spending up to a third of their lives in jobs that don't inspire them, in workplaces where they don't feel valued or that they matter, and in an environment where they are stressed and don't feel psychologically safe.

A lack of effective and inspirational leadership is at the heart of this problem.

I am striving to create a world where people love their jobs again.

Challenging the Status Quo

Throughout this book you will hear the call to action to "challenge the status quo." What does that mean?

To challenge the status quo we must stop, reflect, and rethink. We must not just do things because that is "the way they have always been done." Challenging the status quo means to critically assess whether our leadership practices are effective and working, to change things up when they are not working or serving us.

Thinking on leadership has not maintained pace with a rapidly changing world. It is time to rethink conventional approaches to people leadership and leadership training. I believe in a growth mindset and using self-awareness, self-reflection, and emotional intelligence to continually improve ourselves and our leadership style.

This book is the first in a series that will serve to do that, to challenge your thinking about leadership. To challenge you to transform to be the best leader you can be. Someone that inspires others into meaningful action, someone that attracts talented people to work with you on your vision and mission, someone that other leaders look up to and admire.

What will this book do for you?

As we embark on this journey together, I want to share my experiences and help you to discover all of the people-leadership skills that you were not taught in school.

I will provide guidance on how you can adopt self-reflection as a powerful tool to develop your growth mindset so you become a great and inspiring leader. A leader that is continually learning and refining your leadership style.

I trust you will enjoy this book and find it valuable. If you would like to learn more about The Leadership Project, if you have questions you would like answered, or any feedback on the book, we would love to hear from you.

How to use this book

How can you make the most of this book so you can become the best leader you can be? The leader that others willingly follow?

To make this book useful for you, I encourage you to:

- Keep an open mind
- Be ready to unlearn what you think you already know
- Commit to a learning mindset
- Answer the self-reflection questions at the end of each chapter

At the end of each chapter, take notes. Give yourself an honest scorecard of how well you apply the concepts in this book. Consider what action you could take to continue to improve and learn.

Remember to learn something new every day, unlock the power of self-reflection, and always challenge the status quo.

Reach out to The Leadership Project at www.mickspiers.com where you can download our self-reflection journal and some great resources to help you put the concepts in this book into practice.

Chapter One

Excitement and Anxiety

Euphoric disorientation

Congratulations! You have finally been recognized. Senior leadership saw something special in you. They saw your potential, they saw your prowess. You have been acknowledged for all of your hard work and have been rewarded with that promotion you have been craving. So, "You're a leader, now what?"

It is an almost universal truth that all newly appointed leaders go through the same journey and pattern. This is a story that repeats itself across all types of organizations and all industries. You are most likely extremely good at what you do. You may be a great accountant, a great software engineer, a great digital marketing associate. Unfortunately, being great at your chosen profession does not automatically mean that you will find success and become a great leader of *people*. And so, your journey to becoming a leader begins.

A Mixture of Emotions

You are experiencing a mixture of emotions right now. You are floating on a cloud of euphoric excitement. Feelings of pride and joy welling up inside you. You're wanting to tell everyone who will listen (and maybe some who won't) that you finally have that promotion you deserve.

These feelings will be reinforced by a flood of messages from people congratulating you on your success. Your parents, your partner, your colleagues, your new peers, your boss, all telling you how proud they are and congratulating you on your success.

Then comes the thud. You crash back down to earth. Tomorrow brings a new day and it is back to business as usual. Business as usual for everyone. Everyone except for you.

On the morning of your first day as a leader, or perhaps even the night before, this is when the anxiety starts to creep in.

The euphoria of yesterday is now forgotten. People aren't talking about your promotion anymore. They are ready to get back to work. Your amazing news is no longer newsworthy.

This is when you start to realise that no one has ever taken the time to show you what it means to be a leader. You feel lost and do not know where to start.

In some people, these feelings will manifest in "Imposter Syndrome" where you start questioning your own rite of passage. People experiencing this will ask themselves:

- "What is so special about me?"
- "Why would people follow me as a leader?"
- "Who am I to think I can lead other people?"

Please take some comfort that you are not alone. Imposter Syndrome is very common in any career transition. I will be providing key learnings and concepts in this book to help you conquer that anxiety and kick Imposter Syndrome to the curb.

What got you here won't get you to where you want to be

You will soon discover that the skills and qualities that got you to this point will not be the same ones you need to be successful in your new role. In some cases they may even hold you back.

You will start to uncover that leadership, and human beings, are far more complex than you ever imagined. You may even start questioning whether or not leadership is for you. You may have fleeting moments where you yearn for returning back to your familiar comfort zone of spreadsheets, programming, graphic design, or whatever your tools of craft were.

In this case, please be patient with yourself and show self-compassion. As with any new skill, it takes time to build. It will come. I will show you in this book the path to accelerate your development as a high-performance leader. Leadership is a skill that can be learned and is something you can continue to improve on.

A Deluge of Firsts

During these first pivotal weeks and months as a leader, you will go through a deluge of firsts: Your first time leading a team meeting. First time having to make a critical decision that impacts you and the team. First time you have conflict in the team that you are expected to resolve. First time sitting at the leadership table with your new peers in front of your new boss. First time in a job interview where you are the interviewer instead of the interviewee. First time trying to manage the team's budget. First time that one of your team members starts behaving erratically and you don't know why. First time having to give someone feedback. First time doing performance reviews. The list goes on.

The typical scenario is that you get thrown in the deep end of the pool and are expected to sink or swim. To take the job interview example, it is not uncommon for you to be told you are sitting on a panel interview this Thursday morning and be given no instructions on what to do. Instead you are just given a bunch of resumes to review.

Compounding workload

It is not uncommon at this point for your workload to compound and become unmanageable. Many new leaders find themselves leaning back and still doing large chunks of their old job while still trying to come to grips with their new responsibilities. This can be for a number of reasons. You could be just craving familiar ground, you may be struggling with directing your team on how to do your former job, or you may be just trying to prove yourself. In any case, this approach is setting you up for a fall. It will start to impact your work/life balance. You will find yourself working longer hours than ever before, and you may feel the weight of the world on your shoulders. Every day is bringing you new problems to manage. Furthermore, you may be getting less recognition than you previously received as expectations have shifted. You are a leader now and people are expecting "more" of you.

No one to talk to

To compound your anxiety and ever-increasing workload, you feel that you have no one you can talk to. Depending on the relationship you have with your new boss and the environment you work in, you may feel that you cannot raise your hand and ask for help. You may feel that admitting you are lost and that you need guidance is some sort of confession that you don't know what you are doing. That you never deserved the promotion in the first place.

It is normal, you are normal

While none of the above situations should be the case, I want you to know that these feelings you are experiencing are normal. Nearly every leader in the world goes through a similar experience when they first become a leader.

The common path - mimicking those before you

The way many, or even most, new leaders learn their craft in leadership is suboptimal. Many are left to fend for themselves with little or no support, training, or coaching.

Formal leadership training is typically reserved for senior managers and executive leadership. This training comes at a time in their career when poor leadership habits have already been formed. Ingrained habits become increasingly harder to break. Furthermore, many of these formal programs teach outdated techniques and use ineffective training methods.

Please note, some of these programs are exceptionally good. I have been blessed to have the opportunity to go through transformational programs under the expert tutelage of amazing people like Dr. Melinda Muth. However, I cannot give the same badge of transformational quality to all of the programs I see in the market.

In the absence of access to quality programs, the new leader looks to other sources of information and knowledge. They may revert to YouTube and Google for answers. They will look at mimicking the behaviors of other leaders around them. In both of these cases this is a hit-or-miss affair. If they are lucky enough to find good resources and good role models to follow then they are in good shape. However, this is often not the case.

Some organizations will also appoint the new leader with a mentor. Another hit-or-miss affair. The mentor will typically not have any formal training on how to be a mentor and will be sharing their own leadership thoughts (which may be good, bad, or a mixture).

The Influential Mindset

This may all seem daunting right now. I want you to take comfort that there are ways for you to fast track through this difficult phase in your career. You can come out the other end as a great leader.

Leadership can be taught, it is not something you are just born with.

The lessons in this book are designed to help you discover what leadership is really about. To shift to an Influential Mindset. To provide practical guidance you can put into action.

The Influential Mindset is based on an understanding the psychology of how people learn, understanding how people make decisions, asking insightful questions, elevating your deep listening skills, becoming an inspirational communicator, unlocking your emotional intelligence. Also stepping into a high-performance mindset, inspiring your team to achieve great feats, unlocking emerging properties so your team is greater than the sum of its parts, and getting your team to work with you with all of their heart and soul, not just for a paycheck.

The chapters in this book will help you to understand what it really means to be a leader. How to become a leader that people will willingly follow anywhere. How to influence and inspire people into meaningful action. How to become the leader you wish you always had. How to attract and retain an amazing team around you. To delegate with ease and free up your time. How to develop a high-performance team that fires on all cylinders. How to be further recognized and rewarded as you become a great leader.

Once you make this shift to an Influential Mindset, you can achieve almost anything as a leader. You will find your purpose and meaning. You will multiply your personal impact on the world through your ability to inspire and influence those around you. You will walk through the world with more confidence and poise every day.

A great responsibility

At all times remember the responsibility that comes with being a leader. As Zach Mercurio beautifully described during his interview on The Leadership Project podcast [2], "As a leader you are responsible for the place where your team are spending a third of their lives." This is a responsibility that you must take seriously. There is a lot at stake here. The environment you create will have a long and lasting impact on almost every part of their life. If they are unhappy at work, it will inevitably impact their home lives, the way that they see and value themselves, and their general level of happiness and outlook in life.

Things you must know

Some things that you must know before we start: there is no silver bullet here. Leadership is something that you must work on every day. You must be willing to put in the work. You must be willing to unlearn what you think you already know. You must keep an open mind with an abundance of curiosity. You also need to ensure you have the right motives for why you want to be a leader in the first place.

The Proven Path to High-Performance Leadership

As we work through this, I will show you the proven path to high-performance leadership by committing to your values, conquering your anxieties, unlocking an Influential Mindset, multiplying your impact, and continuously developing your leadership through coaching and self-reflection.

A moment of self-reflection

Take a moment now to stop, think, and reflect on your own experience in the transition to leadership:

1. Are you experiencing this mixture of emotions from euphoric excitement to anxiety and feeling lost?
2. How do you approach things when you are doing things for the very first time?
3. What have been your sources of information to learn from?
4. Do you feel confident in sticking your hand up and asking for help?
5. Is your workload compounding?
6. Are you mimicking the behaviors of leaders before you (the good and the bad)?
7. Do you understand the responsibility of a leader?
8. Are you ready to shift your mindset?
9. Are you ready and committed to put in the work?
10. Are you ready to unlearn what you think you already know?

Chapter Two

What is a Leader?

Thinking back to one of the greatest successes of my career, there is one personal achievement that I will always be proud of, one with so many lessons learned as a leader.

In late 2009, I was greatly honored to be selected to become the Global Project Director of $150M+ project in Auckland, New Zealand. In this role I was to be the leader of a large global team spread from Paris to Hong Kong to Sydney to Auckland. I would lead a multinational development across four countries, time zones, and cultures. To this date, this is the single most successful project delivery I have been involved in.

However, I also made many mistakes along the way. Over those years of the project, I would become the "go-to" person for most topics. If there was a technical or engineering issue, "ask Mick" what do we need to do to meet the next milestone? "Ask Mick" how are we running financially? "Ask Mick" what is the customer's preference on this key topic? "Ask Mick." I did have a wonderful team with me, but I had structured things in a way where I was the key interface for almost any topic. The end result was that I worked 14–16 hours per day for a number of years and the project was delivered on time and under budget. It was a very proud moment on the morning of go-live. A sign of just how "hands-on" I had become is that I stayed up all night the day before launch, making sure everything was spot on, and was at Britomart railway station at 5:12am on a crispy cold Auckland morning to watch the very first paying customer come through the gates.

At the time, I did not have enough self-awareness to know where I had gone wrong as a leader, but this soon became clear.

After a period of time, I wanted to move back to Australia and did so with a promotion to boot. The problem truly kicked in within a short number of weeks. I would need to return to Auckland just one month later.

The team did their best and they were amazing. There were just too many things that were sitting at my feet, sitting in my mind, that I was doing every day and every week. Many of these things were topics I was handling on autopilot, I knew what needed to be done and I was just doing it. In addition, the customer had become very reliant on this and it was a big adjustment for them. Furthermore, there were the teams in Paris, Hong Kong, and Sydney that had also become accustomed to me being that main interface on many topics.

When I returned to Auckland, I took a completely different approach. From that moment onward, I did not do anything in isolation. For every task I was either coaching or training someone else. I was shadowing them as they did it themselves. Then transitioned to them doing it without the need for me to be in the room.

It took the next eight months before I could return to Australia and without the need to Yo-Yo back to New Zealand.

The lessons I had learned were deep and stay with me until this very day. I had gathered an incredibly talented team around me. Some amazing people like Neil George, Gabriel Gonzalez, Greg Patterson, Alessandra Cadness, and Bruce Hunter to name just a few. However, I had not effectively engaged, empowered, and energized them throughout the project. By becoming the "Go-To" person on most topics I had not enabled them for their own success. Success as individuals and success for the project after my departure. I had developed a level of dependence where I was the bottleneck and choke point.

I am pleased to report that, despite my initial failings as a leader, Neil and Gabriel in particular have gone on to forge very successful careers as leaders themselves.

Differences between Managers and Leaders

To be clear, there is a time, a place, and a need for management and managers, but it is fundamentally different to being a leader. It is important to note that people can be both. They can be both manager and leader and can adopt the right style for the right moment and task.

To help solidify the difference, consider that it is very possible to be a great leader and not good at managing or to be an excellent manager without being a great leader. When you find someone that has the balance of both, you have someone very special.

A manager tells people what to do and how to do it. A manager will typically focus on the performance of their direct reports and be focused on results and outcomes. They will oversee day-to-day activities and be monitoring "To-Do" or task lists. A manager typically becomes personally connected to their projects. They often treat the project like "their baby." In many respects, the project is more important to them than their team members. This is exactly what I did when I was in Auckland, I became laser focused on project performance, took full accountability for everything, and treated everything like it was my own. The project result was amazing, but this was at the expense of the development of the team around me. It was detrimental to my own health and wellbeing. To be clear, without any attention to being a manager, teams can drift and not be focused on outcomes such as project delivery and completion, on managing costs, and managing schedules. So management and managers are essential.

Conversely, a leader is more focused on inspiring people into action. A leader will be able to inspire people to do something because they *want* to do it, because they saw the bigger picture of why it was important, and not simply because the boss *told* them to do it.

A leader will be less focussed on the day-to-day action list and more focused on the overall vision.

Leaders are generally able to strategize and have a broader lens on what is happening rather than being focused on the immediate project. This will typically result in finding more innovative ways of achieving the outcomes they are seeking to achieve.

Another key attribute is about coaching. It is often said that if you give someone a fish they will eat for a day, but if you teach someone to (sustainably) fish they will eat for a lifetime. This is 100 percent true in a team leadership role. A great leader will often take on the role of coach and develop those around them. A great leader develops other great leaders.

One of the key mistakes that many new leaders make is to become the oracle of knowledge within their team. If you become the answer to every question we have a problem. If your team's default is to "ask Julie" then you are not teaching or coaching people to think for themselves or to solve their own problems.

One of the key attributes of coaching is the ability to ask more questions than give answers. This gives people the space to grow and learn. When people have to think and find answers themselves it triggers new synapses in the brain and new learnings. If they discover the answer on their own they will have a much greater probability of retaining that new knowledge and develop their own problem-solving skills. A great example of this is the "Extreme Question Experiment" from Liz Wiseman [3]. This is where the leader, for an entire day, only asks questions instead of providing any answers, and it can have surprising results.

A leader is also able to look at any situation through multiple perspectives. They will understand a problem through the perspective of other stakeholders including customers and other teams. They will consider the broader implications for the entire organization, whereas a manager will typically be focused on questions like "what does this mean for me?" or "What does this mean for my project?"

Leaders will have an innovative mindset. They will be willing to unlearn what they think they already know. They will be able to deeply listen to their team and a situation. This means not just listening for what you already know, or listening for what you want to hear, but also really listening to what is going on from multiple perspectives. They will consider multiple options for how an outcome can be realized rather than being focused on one path or one set of actions. Leaders think in the "Art of the possible" and consider why something *can* be done rather than why something *can't* be done. This does not mean that they do not have their eyes wide open for risks, issues, challenges, or roadblocks. Rather, the leader will be able to see with every risk also comes opportunity and consider how to mitigate that risk or turn it into something advantageous. The leader will foresee issues, challenges, and roadblocks and help their team to navigate around those or remove them altogether. One of the key reasons for a leader to have a strong network is to help with the removal of roadblocks.

Leaders will typically speak in language of future tense and be focused on the opportunities in front of the team rather than speaking in past or present tense. This does not mean forgetting the lessons of the past, but does mean being focused on what is in front of the team. A great leader realizes that you cannot change what has already happened, you can only control what you do from this moment onward. So, learn from the past, and focus on the future.

A great leader needs to be able to balance between being decisive and being flexible. Leaders need to be able to bring in multiple viewpoints, be considerate, and then decisive to ensure there is a clear path forward. But then also be flexible enough to be able to pivot and change course if circumstances change or new information comes to the fore. Unfortunately, I have had a number of leaders in the past that have been too overly stubborn to the point where they will not change their mind even when overwhelming evidence indicates we need to change direction. Their mindset is that if they "change their mind" that this is a sign of being a weak leader or being indecisive, but this is not the case. People will respect a change in course that is based on a reasoned understanding that the context or environment changed. The demise of companies like Kodak and Blockbuster come to mind when I think of this, but I am sure you all can think of your own examples of this.

A great leader takes the time to truly know their team and treats everyone with respect and dignity as individuals. A manager will typically treat everyone as equals, which can be admirable, but is not the best way to develop and nurture the individuals in your team. A leader has the ability to help someone identify their own individual superpowers and to coach them to unleash that talent for the greater cause and vision. They will connect with staff with genuine curiosity to discover these talents and ask smart questions to help them do so.

MICK SPIERS

A great leader empowers, enables and energizes their team to allow them the space to be successful. Empowerment needs to be at the lowest possible level in the team structure while still getting the job done, Enablement is being able to give the team the tools and resources they need to be successful, and Energizing is the motivation and inspiration to the common cause that results in people lifting their performance to new levels, individually and collectively.

This concept of the 3Es (Empowerment, Enablement, and Energizing) is brilliantly described in the ground-breaking book *All In: How the Best Managers Create a Culture of Belief and Drive Big Results* [4] from Adrian Gostick and Chester Elton.

A great leader develops a blame-free culture and a psychologically safe environment for people to grow and learn. A blame-free culture is based on a learning mindset. The mindset that there is "no such thing as failure, only learning." This will drive a culture of openness and transparency where people are not afraid to speak up if a mistake has been made. A psychologically safe environment is one where people are not afraid to speak up if they disagree with the current course of action. For the good of the team you need diversity of thought and the freedom for people to speak their mind if they see something the leader has not.

A psychologically safe environment is one where people are not afraid to speak up when they need help. The term resilience is often seen as a positive, but in my view can be dangerous. The sometimes-stated desire for people to be resilient can result in people being too afraid to put up their hand and say that they do not understand what they are supposed to be doing or are drowning and need support. Asking for help should be seen as a sign of strength, not a sign of weakness, and we need to encourage people to do so—early and often.

We do want people to build their resilience, but we do not want the word resilience to become a cover for poor workplace behaviors (like bullying) or setting the wrong expectation. Statements like "You just need to become more resilient" are generally unhelpful, they are dismissive of what a person may be going through and feeling, and can set poor expectations.

In discussing this topic with Jo Lanigan, a Master Certified Coach with Coach Masters Academy, she provided a great insight that we should be striving for "transparent resilience." The concept here is to encourage people to build their personal resilience to challenging situations, but to do so with dialogue and discussion where you can safely and openly discuss it.

Another avenue where the word resilience can be positive is when it comes to team resilience. A resilient team is one that rallies around a team member that is struggling at that moment in time. They could be struggling with something in their personal life or struggling with their work or their workload and a great team will support them through that time.

A great leader is able to balance between being strong and being vulnerable. Vulnerability is a very admirable trait that people deeply respect. The leader, at the end of the day, is a human being themselves and not some sort of superhero. A deeply respected leader is someone who is intellectually humble and openly discusses their strengths and weaknesses. A wonderful lesson I took from John C. Maxwell was the story of an executive leader who challenged John on this concept saying that admitting your failures and shortcomings is a sign of weakness. The simple answer from John was "You are assuming that they don't already know." People and teams can be very astute at understanding their leaders' virtues and weaknesses, sometimes even before the leader has achieved self-awareness. Therefore, being open and transparent about your weaknesses establishes great trust and enables the team to work with that. A great leader will surround themselves with people that they know, like, and trust that can cover these areas of weakness for the greater good. There is not a single leader on earth that can be good at everything. Acknowledging that is a great step in your own future development.

A leader inspires people into action. A great leader inspires people to achieve great things because *they want to do it*, not because they were *told* to do it. Along the way they will develop a great deal of ownership and buy-in from the team. This is critical in developing long-term sustainable growth. When someone has buy-in and ownership they will remember what they learned along the way. They will become champions and force multipliers for the vision of the organization.

A truly great leader is someone that then develops other leaders. Taking the time to coach and mentor others to also become exceptional and inspirational leaders.

My Journey as a Leader

The truth is that I have been very fortunate to find myself in leadership roles from early on in my life. This does not mean I was always a great leader. It is something that I have worked on throughout my life. Learning from successes and failures along the way.

"Lifelong leaders are lifelong learners." - Sean Cannell.

In 2013, after returning from Auckland to Sydney, I was appointed to my first executive-level role. This was far from my first leadership role, but was my first role sitting at "the big table." I was to have my own multi-million division and would sit on the executive of a billion-dollar company.

There are many things from that experience that I will never forget, but two in particular are stand-out moments.

My CEO, Chris Jenkins, is still to this day one of the greatest leaders I have ever had the pleasure of working with and for. I am certain even as I start this manuscript that I will reference Chris multiple times for the things I learned from him.

Upon my appointment, and immediately prior to my first executive meeting, he pulled me aside and told me something I will never forget:

"You have made it, but never think that you've made it." - Chris Jenkins

As he continued to explain his riddle, the importance of these words started to sink in. It was about being humble and not becoming arrogant. This was perfect coming from him as he is both of those things.

The other powerful message was to continue to learn every single day. Learn from those around you, learn from your peers, learn from your staff, and never think you know everything.

The second memorable moment was a truly transformative event in my career. I was afforded the opportunity to choose my first executive coach. The process involved interviewing three different coaches. I was to pick the person that would become my guide and confidant in that critical first year of my transition into executive leadership.

Of the three coaches, two of them were like 20-years-older versions of myself. They had similar backgrounds and were from similar industries. The third coach, Joy Pitts, was nothing like me at all. This was perhaps my first foray into understanding the importance of diversity of thought. If I picked either of the first two, I am sure I still would have achieved great results and had an acceleration of the path I was already on. However, I decided to go with Joy with the goal of challenging and broadening my perspective.

This is without doubt one of the smartest decisions I have made in my career. Something I will never regret. Joy took me on a journey of self-discovery. I learned many things about myself as well as important lessons on leadership along the way.

One of the techniques that Joy taught me, that I still use to this day, is about the power of self-reflection.

Each day after work, I practice going through the following five questions:

1. What worked well today?
2. What didn't go well?
3. What would I do differently next time?
4. What did I learn from and about others today?
5. What did I learn about myself?

It is this self-reflection practice that underpins my daily and continual learning. It inspired the self-reflection questions in this book and the development of the Self Reflection Journal. You can download your copy of the journal at www.mickspiers.com

My journey as a leader has continued to flourish since those days. I have gone on to lead increasingly larger businesses. I led the Ground Transportation Systems business for Thales in Australia and New Zealand.

I moved to Hong Kong to lead Asia Pacific for Thales Revenue Collection Systems. Have been involved in mergers & acquisitions. Shifted to Singapore to lead Cubic Transportation Systems in Asia. Shifted to leading global business units. I have launched multiple new businesses including the launch of Umo Mobility for Cubic. I have led pivotal global functions including Strategy & Marketing. All of these experiences have made up the fabric of who I am as a person and the leader I have become. Learning every day from those around me and from each experience, success, and failure along the way.

A dawning moment of realization

There are moments that can change the course of your life forever; moments that bring brilliant flashes of self-awareness that once seen can never be unseen.

One of these moments in my life came at the retirement party of a dear colleague that I will be eternally grateful for.

Bob Hamilton is a legend in the industry of smart mobility and mobility payments. His work, together with his long-time business partner Gary Yamamura, fundamentally changed the way that Automated Fare Collection systems are delivered. Shifting a very conventional and conservative industry from a project-oriented world to a Platform as a Service model.

At Bob's retirement party he made a speech that included one sentence that would go on to change my life and my perspective forever. One of his remarks on his career was that "it took 40 years for him to find the best leader he had worked with" and he was referring to me. This shook me to my core in the most powerful and positive way. I was gobsmacked and felt 10 feet tall at that moment.

In the ensuing weeks, I spoke to many friends in our industry. I was still riding on a cloud from Bob's powerful words but all the time with self-doubt and disbelief. I was sharing the story with them: "You are not going to believe what Bob Hamilton said at his retirement." The resounding response from everyone I shared this story with was "D'uh, Mick, that's what you do!"

These events put me into a state of self-reflection for several weeks. Up until this point I had always put my success as a leader down to technical prowess. I had thought that people respected me for my technical knowledge and expertise. I was a thought leader in our industry. The more I reflected, the more I researched, the more clear the realization became. I had been successful in my career due to my ability to inspire people into great and meaningful action. To inspire them through clarity of vision and purpose. To attract people around me that believed in the same things I did; to influence them, to coach and mentor them, to help them uncover their own superpowers and strengths. To help them discover themselves and learn about themselves every day. To take the time to get to truly know who they are and what makes them tick. To treat them the way they wanted to be treated. To give them the space to grow and become the best version of themselves they can be. To give them purpose and meaning in what they do. To ensure their voice is heard and their opinions valued. To treat them like they matter.

I had been successful through relationships and how I related to others. The true secret to leadership.

I had developed an influential mindset without being consciously aware of it. This influential mindset was the key to my success.

Common Knowledge is not Common Practice

I continued to research leadership. I continued the search to understand where my success as a leader had come from.

Realizations would continue to flood in. All of my formative years as a leader learning from Chris Jenkins, Melinda Muth, Joy Pitts, Millar Crawford, Ross Nicol, Kim Hall, and many others had forged a set of values and practices as a leader that I found to be completely natural.

The danger of this is the assumption that if it is natural to you, then it must be common. Everyone must know this; everyone must be doing this.

The deeper I looked into the field of leadership the more I found that common knowledge is not common at all. If it is common knowledge it is certainly not common practice. Countless stories of horrible bosses and terrible leaders demotivating their teams and creating uninspiring and stressful work environments. In most cases through lack of knowledge, training, and skills on what it takes to be a leader. If you are one of the many people in the world that are suffering from working in a place with poor leadership, always remember not to put down to malice what could be more easily explained as incompetence. The vast majority of leaders have their heart in the right place, they have just never been shown the way.

The Birth of The Leadership Project

It was from these realizations and research that led me to found The Leadership Project. It started simply as a podcast where I wanted to bring together people from diverse backgrounds to share their wisdom, insights, and perspectives. To challenge the status quo of what it meant to be a leader.

Over the course of a year this turned from side project to passion to healthy obsession. During that time I would continue to research leadership and broaden my horizons. I would undergo training and certification as a coach with Coach Masters Academy under the incomparable Dr. Ben Koh and his amazing faculty of ICF certified leaders and coaches. I would spend all of my spare time researching, discussing, coaching, and podcasting all about leadership.

The amazing revelation in all of this was the discovery of joy. Whenever I was in this leadership space, I would find myself in a flow state. A state where time seemed immaterial. A state of everlasting, renewable, and sustainable happiness. A state where my heart and soul were constantly glowing in the basking warmth that comes from helping others achieve their full potential.

Over that period of time this passion became impossible to ignore. I made a step that many would consider bold and courageous. A step that was clear and obvious to me. I would turn my back on an incredibly successful corporate career. Turning my back at potentially the peak of my career. I would dedicate the remainder of my professional life to improving the state of leadership in the world, to addressing the leadership crisis.

The Leadership Project went from a side passion project to a full-blown leadership academy. I would grow a team to multiply my impact on the world. We would launch cohort-based courses that were based on the science of how people learn, embracing techniques such as collaborative (or social) learning, micro learning, and gamification. Techniques that are proven to have a transformative and sustainable impact on our students, enabling them to put great leadership into meaningful action, rather than just pass on knowledge that may or may not be put into action when they return to their workplace. We would deliver transformative coaching services (one-on-one and group coaching) to help people discover themselves as leaders. We would help businesses to forge high-performance teams. Helping them to form, storm, norm, and perform as a team. In some cases this would be remediation work. Helping them to re-form, re-storm, re-norm, re-perform, and re-find their former glory as a team.

Team Leadership is not for everyone

An interesting thing happens in many, or even most, people's careers. At some point early in your working life you are identified and noticed for your talents. Senior management may have even used words like *"Jill is showing real potential as a future leader"* on the back of some form of technical prowess you are showing. You may be the best app developer, the best financial analyst, the best digital marketer, etc., the company has seen in a very long time. However, being the best at your chosen craft or domain does not automatically mean that you have the skills required to be successful as a leader.

You may also find that you do not enjoy leadership. It is just not your thing.

When this happens, we end up with a compounding effect. The individual gets stressed and unmotivated as they are no longer enjoying their work. We end up with a poor leader in a pivotal role in the organization and we lose our best individual contributor in their chosen domain (software engineer, digital marketing, nursing, etc.).

Why is it so hard?

The simple answer is that human beings are complex. For most people, their chosen domain and craft is normally based on known and repeatable rules and truths. If you are an engineer you have the laws of physics and mathematics to fall back on. Generally results are predictable and repeatable. If you are in finance you have accounting rules and practices and tools you can generally rely on. Even with emerging and seemingly complex fields like machine learning, you are still dealing with mostly definable and known variables and constraints.

Human beings are vastly different to this. There are more than 7 billion people on the planet and no two are the same. What works for, and inspires, one person may have the complete opposite effect on the next. Furthermore, even the same person can react differently to the same situation depending on a wide range of factors including what is happening in their home or family life, their level of stress, and many others. This means that people that you will be asked to lead and manage are not necessarily predictable and repeatable at all.

People have physiological and psychological needs. Some of these are stated needs, but the vast majority are unstated. People are emotional and generally speaking make emotional rather than rational decisions, even if they justify those decisions rationally.

One of the biggest misnomers in the world is the use of the phrases "Hard Skills" meaning technical domain skills and "Soft Skills" referring to the less tangible elements managing people. Nothing could be further from the truth. The so-called "Soft Skills" are generally much harder to master for most people. I would much prefer to see us use terms such as "Domain Skills" specific to a particular profession or trade and "Core Skills" referring to skills that are pervasive across any industry or domain.

If you are one of those people that have found the transition from individual contributor to leader or manager to be challenging, please take comfort that you are not alone. I have had countless experiences in my career of watching new leaders go through that journey of self-discovery.

Not taught at school

One of the underlying problems is that these "Core Skills" are not taught in the majority of curricula in schools, colleges, or universities. These institutions typically focus on domain knowledge and skills. The better ones also teach people to have critical reasoning skills.

Many educational systems are based around examinations with pass/fail criteria where there are right and wrong answers. This is not necessarily conducive to people management where there is no single correct answer to any situation or problem.

When people enter the workforce their academic knowledge is reinforced with some level of practical training on "how to" do a certain activity. Training people on how to use tools, training on organization process on "how things are done here."

When it comes to leadership or managerial roles, most people are just thrown in the deep end and expected to sink or swim. For example, people are not always taught how to manage performance or conduct performance appraisals before the first time they have to do it. New leaders find themselves in a recruitment situation interviewing potential candidates without ever having done it before. Only relying on their experiences from when they were a candidate themselves. Managing conflict between two staff members without any training in conflict management. Chairing their first team meeting without having training on how to prepare and conduct an effective meeting. Looking to inspire their team without training on how to do so. And the list goes on.

Specialist vs Generalist

Team leadership is not necessarily for everyone. There are many people that cultivate amazingly successful careers from being an absolute expert in their chosen field and may never take on a managerial role. There is absolutely nothing wrong with that. In some cases they could go on to change the world and win Nobel prizes for their work.

A call-out to all leaders of organizations would be to assess if you are creating an environment where people can thrive as a specialist. In many organizations it is widely accepted that the only way to get ahead and be promoted and rewarded is through becoming a leader of increasingly larger teams and portfolios. I would strongly argue that this should not be the case. I encourage organizations to consider what reward, recognition, and promotion scheme can be put in place to support and encourage the development of technical specialists who do not wish to have a people leadership role. This could be a scheme that runs in parallel to the leadership path. Have a path that allows a deep specialist to progress in their career without needing to take on leadership roles if it is not a good fit for them.

IBM sets a good example here with their system of "IBM fellows." To be an IBM fellow you are at the pinnacle of experts in your chosen field and people are inspired and motivated to become recognized as a fellow.

My personal experience was to take the generalist path leading increasingly larger teams. As a generalist, rather becoming a deep specialist in one field, I spent time in a variety of fields. Prior to entering the executive ranks I performed in a wide range of diverse roles including engineering, training, quality management, bid management, project management, sales, and marketing. I found this to be very rewarding. This path set me up for success as I moved into executive management roles with profit & loss accountability. I am acutely aware that this is not the only viable path, and I do encourage you to consider this on your journey. Do you want to be a deep expert recognized as a specialist in your domain or do you want to follow a generalist path that spans multiple disciplines? There is no right or wrong answer to that.

Leadership is not about you, Leadership is all about you

There are many lessons in this book about how to become a leader or how to become a *better* leader. The one common thread in all of these lessons is that leadership is all about how you relate to other people. A great leader quickly learns that leadership is not about them, it is about the people they are leading, always looking out for their interests, giving them the right environment to thrive, and coaching and nurturing so that they can become the best versions of themselves.

A great leader also soon learns that it is all about them, but not in a self-centred way. As a leader you have a great responsibility. People will be constantly looking to you for signals that everything is okay. Everything you do can have an influence on the ability of the team to perform. You are responsible for the place they are spending up to a third of their lives. It is on you to create an inspiring environment free from undue stress.

Leadership is not about you, it is about your team. Leadership is about your ability to create an amazing and inspiring environment for your team to do their best work.

Mana

When looking at the many great attributes of a great leader there is something that is difficult to describe. In the New Zealand Maori culture they have an amazing term for this, Mana. Mana does not have an immediate translation in English, but can be described in many ways. Picture someone that walks into a crowded room and without saying anything people notice their presence and gravitate toward them. That person is said to have Mana. People will be interested in their views on a variety of topics and will listen intently when they speak. They may not actually say a lot, but when they do speak everyone stops, listens, and reflects. This is not to be confused with people respecting someone because of their position, this is a deeper respect that comes from their feelings and thoughts of them as a person. People with Mana also seem to have a natural ability to relate to, and connect with, anybody. People from all walks of life, all backgrounds, all cultures. Mana could be described as a mixture or presence, composure, respect, and reverence, but once again difficult to fully describe.

I have had a number of leaders in my career that embody this. Chris Jenkins, CEO of Thales Australia, and Millar Crawford are two perfect examples of this. Consider now whether you have experienced similar people that embody these attributes, as they will become great reference points for your own learnings as a leader.

Are leaders born or made?

We have all heard the term "born leader" before and it does raise the question as to whether leaders are born. To quote John C. Maxwell, "I have never met one that wasn't." However, jokes aside, it is true that some people have a natural tendency toward leadership based on personality traits, preferences, values, and beliefs. It is equally true that everyone can improve their leadership skill over time. Through a journey of self-discovery and awareness through to application and practice you can continually improve your leadership. Great leaders are also great learners. They are open minded and constantly learn new things and remain adaptable to a changing world.

Planning your own succession

One of the key objectives of any leader is to develop their team around them until the point where they are no longer needed.

This advice may surprise some. I encourage you to be planning for your own succession and to do so early and often. Start looking around and see what leadership talent exists in the team. It may be untapped and unseen talent that people have not noticed before.

You may be feeling instantly worried about this. You may be asking questions like "What if they rise higher and faster than me?" or "What if the team does not need me anymore?"

Some leaders may become concerned about this and their own status.

You may feel threatened by those coming through that may have greater skills and potential than themselves.

There are many great reasons why you should start your own succession planning immediately.

People will greatly respect that you have invested your time in the personal and professional development of your team. That person that you nurtured will also become your great ally in the future, even if they do rise to higher heights than you.

Developing the team around you takes pressure off your own workload. Having people that you can trust to get on with managing (or leading) key aspects of the team and the work gives you thinking time so that you can focus on the vision and the road ahead and gives you time back. You may even be able to get some of that elusive work/life balance that you desire.

If nothing else, you will find that having a successor will enable you new opportunities to move on to the next big thing when it arises. Giving you the opportunity for your next promotion or lateral move on to something interesting and challenging. If you have become the sole focal point of your team and a single point of failure, it makes it that much more difficult for your senior leadership to find new opportunities for you in your career.

Planning for succession should take on a few different perspectives. The first is to consider who would be your "go-to" person (or people) in the event that you go on vacation or have a period of illness. Some would also call this the dreaded "what if you got hit by a bus?" scenario, which is not nice to think of, but is still important to consider.

Then start looking in horizons of one-to-three-year periods. Look across the business and see who would be ready for your role in one year's time, who would be ready in three years' time. Interestingly, the answer may be different depending on that time period. You also do not need to limit yourself to your immediate team, there may be someone from a cross-functional team that may show the attitude and aptitude to be your successor and would gain great benefit from a lateral or diagonal move.

Once you have your thoughts gathered, do not be shy about sharing your thoughts with your HR Business Partner and your own boss to see if they have a different perspective. Remember diversity of thought is always good and they may see things that you are not seeing. From your shortlist of possible successors then start considering what developmental needs these future leaders may have. Start implementing a strategy to help them address those needs through a combination of on-the-job experiences, mentoring, coaching, and formal training (where appropriate). Be careful not to set any explicit expectations with them. It is great to share with them that you see great potential in them and to work on their development, but any explicit statement that they will be your successor can be problematic in the future if things do not pan out as you expected.

Different leaders for different stages of a team

Building on from the discussion on succession, another key lesson that I have learned in my career is that businesses and teams benefit from different types of leaders at different stages in their development and life. The same can also be said for the leader themselves—a leader may need different challenges at different stages of their own personal development.

I have had several instances in my career where I have taken a team's development as far as I could within my areas of expertise and skill. It gets to the point where the team is ready for the next stage in their development and could greatly benefit from the skills and perspectives of a new leader. This could be a successor from within the team, a lateral move from someone else in the organization, or an external candidate coming in with their own unique skills and experiences. This will often coincide with the leader also becoming ready for their next challenge in life and is ready to move on to something that continues their own journey of personal development as a leader.

The team is ready for a new leader, and the leader is ready for a new team.

Some examples from my own journey. One of the key and proud moments in my career was the launch of the platform business within Cubic

Transportation System and the launch of a new B2C brand called Umo. Cubic, at the time, was a relatively traditional and large engineering firm with 50 years' experience in delivering large-scale engineering projects to some of the world's most iconic cities. They had delivered public transport ticketing systems into London (the famous Oyster card), New York (Metrocard), Sydney (Opal), San Francisco (Clipper), Brisbane (Go Card), Chicago (Ventra), and the list goes on. These were mostly traditional projects delivered using base products but with a heavy amount of customization and bespoke development to meet the needs of these large (or even Mega) cities. Cubic has subsequently been going through a transformation to a product-oriented organization under the strong executive leadership of Jeff Lowinger and the technical leadership of Galen Chui. A transformation that is proving very successful with a streamlining and synchronization of products delivering greater outcomes in terms of speed to market, competitiveness and profitability. This benefits both Cubic and its customers.

The platforms business (Umo) was something very unique for Cubic. We had come to the realization that the traditional project approach and the use of large-scale individual systems was inaccessible to cities and towns that were more in the small to mid-sized market. We therefore developed a strategy based on the development of a multi-tenant platform where, instead of each city having their own system, there would be a single instance of the platform that towns and cities of all sizes could consume and use in an as-a-service model. The Umo platform would also bring forward the need for B2C products in the form of mobile apps, journey planners, and other services that would have a consumer facing brand. Larger cities would typically have their own brand (e.g. Oyster), but smaller to mid-sized cities were more looking for "done-for-you"-type marketing approaches and a brand that they could take straight to their travelers in a direct or co-branded approach. So, on the back of the acquisition of Delerrok (the innovative and groundbreaking company developed by Bob Hamilton and Gary Yamamura), we started to build a suite of platforms that would be everything that a small to mid-sized town would need.

For Cubic, this meant they were going into new territory on multiple fronts. A new market that they had never previously encountered, a new business model (aaS), a new platform architecture, and for the first time a B2C consumer facing brand (Umo).

The birth of this new business required a leader that was focused on setting the overall vision and mission of the business. Defining what the business would become: the values and beliefs, the business model, the growth strategy, innovative new approaches (business and technical), marketing and branding, and bringing a brand-new team together. To add to the complication, we brought this team together during the height of COVID and therefore the majority of this team had never physically met each other and most of the business was conducted over Zoom.

This stage of the business required someone that had strengths in all of these areas, and I was the one chosen to lead and launch the Umo brand and the platforms business.

Over a period of the next 14 months we achieved amazing success even with the cloud of COVID impacting some parts of the business. The launch was very successful and Cubic now has a platform business and a new B2C brand in Umo.

As this matured, it then became obvious that Umo then needed a different type of leader, someone with a more operational focus than a launch focus. This came earlier than originally intended, but it became the right time to transition the business to Bonnie Crawford. From the moment I took on the leadership of the Umo business, I had been working on who would be my most likely successor and had three candidates in mind throughout. For the majority of that time it was not an explicit statement that I was quietly developing these people to be my replacement, but nonetheless I was subtly preparing them from the outset. In this case, I was extremely blessed to have someone as talented as Bonnie on the team, and she immediately started to shine through. I can openly and transparently say that this was one of the easiest transitions I have had as Bonnie came to us with an already well-tuned set of wonderful leadership attributes. Then, when the time came, with Bonnie's amazing strengths and my subtle coaching on a select number of topics, Bonnie was immediately ready to take the reins and the transition was mostly smooth. There are always some areas that do not go perfectly, but this would be the smoothest transition I have experienced in my career. I am now watching with great pride as Bonnie takes the Umo business to new levels. Building on what I had started and then bringing her own strengths and talents to the table. The team was ready for a new leader, and I was ready for a new team.

In parallel to preparing for the transition to Bonnie I had been working with my boss on what options would represent the next logical transition for myself. As Bonnie stepped forward into the Umo role, I went on to be the head of Strategy, Marketing, and Mergers and Acquisitions for the business. This would be a role that played to my individual strengths as well as challenge and stretch me in some new areas for my own personal growth.

The key to this story is to start planning and developing your successor from very early on. When you start out in a new leadership role, you do not really know how soon that transition might happen. Opportunity may come knocking for you to move on to your next challenge, or the team may mature very quickly and be ready for their next leader. If you have not put in the work to develop your successor then the transition is unlikely to go well for anyone at that stage.

Putting It Into Action

There is a lot to consider in this chapter and as you embark on the journey of leadership. It is important to note that there will be different times in your career where you make leadership transitions and you may wish to reconsider the above at these times. Consider what it means to be a leader and whether you are living these behaviors and values. Continue to study those around you and continue to self-reflect on where you are at.

Moment of self-reflection

Take a moment of self-reflection and consider the following:

1. Consider bosses you have had in the past. Were they leaders, were they managers, or a combination of the two? What did you like or dislike about their approaches?
2. Are you focused on the execution of immediate projects and tasks and getting the job done, or do you focus on the bigger picture of what is ahead in the future?
3. Do you inspire people into action because they *want* to do it, or are you simply *telling* people what to do?
4. Do you "*coach*" or do you "*teach*"?
5. Are you a single point of failure that is the oracle of all knowledge in the team?
6. What actions do you take to encourage team members to think for themselves?
7. How do you empower and enable your team members?
8. Have you created a psychologically safe and blame-free environment?
9. Do you know who your possible successor could be? And what are you doing to develop them?

Chapter Three

Taking care of your team

"Leadership is not about being in charge, it is about taking care of those in your charge." - Simon Sinek

A key role for any leader is to take care of their team members. You are responsible for ensuring that everyone in the team feels like they belong. Everyone wants to feel like they matter, feel like they are valued, and feel like their opinions are respected.

A leader has a responsibility for providing a psychologically safe environment where everyone on the team feels free to voice their opinions and contribute without fear of judgment or retribution.

The greatest responsibility of any leader is to take care of your team. Ensuring they are in a good space. Looking out for their physical and mental wellbeing. This means paying close attention and looking out for any signs of stress or uncertainty. Taking the time to take a genuine interest in their wellbeing every single day. Ask them how they are and making sure that they understand that you are genuinely interested in the answer. Keeping an eye out for any behaviors that are "out of their norm." Any form of erratic or out-of-character behavior is usually a good indicator that they are under more stress than normal.

This could be from something in the workplace or something from outside the workplace, but it is still your responsibility to take care no matter the cause.

Some examples of behavior to look for include:

- Extroverts that are all of a sudden very reserved and quiet
- Normally calm people that are having emotional outbursts
- Signs of agitation or irritability

As Zach Mercurio highlighted during his interview on The Leadership Project podcast, "You are responsible for the place where human beings are spending up to a third of their lives." [2]

When someone does show these signs of stress or behavior that is "out of their norm," the best thing you can do as a leader is to explore what is going on. Once again reverting to asking more questions. It could be as simple as asking "Hey, is everything okay?" or "What's on your mind today?"

How are you? Is a question not a greeting

In many societies (and businesses) we have allowed this to creep in. People greet each other in the morning with "How are you?" but use it more like "Hello." If you are going to take the time to ask someone how they are, you need to pause and take a genuine interest in the answer.

This may take some time for your team to get used to. Because of the above-mentioned shift in focus, people have become accustomed to "How are you?" not really being a question, and they will often just say, "Yeah, good," even if that is not really the case.

In the first few weeks of adopting this, you may need to several times follow up with the question "No, really, how are you doing?" After a while they will realize you really want to know, and will be ready to open up to you.

This will be a breakthrough moment for you and your team, and you will be on your way to a relationship based on open and transparent communication. If your team members feel they can really be themselves and tell you how they are feeling, they are then infinitely more likely to share problems with you that you can work on together and/or work on as a whole team. This will uncover underlying issues that may have been dormant and give you the opportunity to address them.

I strongly encourage all of you to take on this challenge. Think about breaking down communication barriers and really listen when you ask your team how they are.

Building an authentic connection

As you take a genuine interest in your team members, you will start to learn much more about them.

This will enable you to develop a deeper connection with them. This will in turn build and maintain a trusted relationship.

When you take the time to learn more about them you will be able to clearly demonstrate to them that you care. Remembering and recalling details and following up with them on how they are going. For example, remembering that their daughter is on her path to soccer stardom, try asking, "Hey Jenny, how did Sarah do with her football trials?" A simple question like this will demonstrate clearly to Jenny that you remembered your last conversation and that she matters to you.

It is critical that this is authentic. People will see straight through you if this is just an act or a show.

Take a moment now to reflect on this in your own career. Do you remember times where a boss or senior person took the time to remember your name, remember something about you, and to make you feel that you matter to them? How did that feel? Can you see the power of doing that with your team and with those you have regular contact with? People always remember these acts of connection.

Enabling their success

Taking care of your team also means setting them up for success. There is almost nothing more frustrating than being held accountable for something that you do not have the support and resources to be successful with.

Enabling your team means to ensure that they have the support that they need to be successful. Empowering them so they can get on with what they do best, giving them the resources and tools they need and removing any roadblocks that are preventing their success.

Always remember that you are paying your team because of their skills and knowledge. It is not logical to pay someone as an expert in their field and then either tell them what to do or not give them the room and resources to get on with their jobs.

A great example of this approach comes from Google and how they train their leaders to ask questions in support of their team members. Google trains leaders around the mantra of having three questions they ask their team members:

1. What are you working on right now?
2. Do you have the resources that you need?
3. Is there anything I can do to help you?

At the root of this is the concept of servant leadership and enabling people to bring their best work forward.

The resources and roadblocks are key here. Remembering that, in your role, you most likely have other connections around the business and a certain amount of influence beyond the sphere of your team. Your team member may need you to go and lobby on the team's behalf for more resources or to garner the support from another team in a different part of the business. It is part of your responsibility to support your team to navigate the business and get the resources and support they need to be successful.

A Psychologically Safe Environment

It is the leader's responsibility to provide their team with a psychologically safe environment.

This is an environment where they feel safe to be able to voice their opinions without fear of judgment or retribution.

This includes giving your team the confidence that they can raise ideas and questions and they can express concerns without fear of punishment or humiliation.

They can be vulnerable and feel safe to raise their hand and ask for help without being perceived as being weak or incompetent.

Importantly, it also enables them to take calculated risks knowing that you have their back.

As Mark Zuckerberg is famous for saying "The biggest risk is not taking any risk." Without psychological safety your team may freeze and not act on opportunities for fear of retribution if they fail.

Some of the best ways you can establish psychological safety is by modeling these behaviors yourself. Be vulnerable. Acknowledge your own mistakes and shortcomings together with the lessons you take from them. When someone is the bearer of bad news, be very conscious of your own reaction. Use active and deep listening and help the person discover their own learnings.

A common misconception of psychological safety is that it is all about having a *soft* environment where it is all love and cuddles. That is not what it is about. Psychological safety is where people can openly (and respectfully) speak their mind and where the reward for doing so is greatly than any fear they might have about speaking up.

Moment of self-reflection

Take a moment now to stop, think, and reflect on the following questions:

1. How well do you know your team and their needs?
2. Do you take the time to get to know them individually?
3. Do you take a genuine interest in their physical and psychological wellbeing?
4. Would you notice any out-of-the-norm behavior?
5. What would you do if you did see that?
6. Have you developed authentic connections with your team?
7. Do you ensure they all know that their opinions are valued?
8. Do you ensure they know they matter to you?
9. Have you created a psychologically safe environment for them?
10. Have you enabled their success?

Chapter Four

Why do you want to be a leader?

Why did you want to become a leader?

We must always remember that leadership is not for everyone. I have encountered many people in my career that have come to this realization. They have tried out leadership for a period of time and discovered that leadership did not sit well with them and/or they were not well suited to having a leadership role.

One such example is Andrew, an extraordinarily talented software architect and engineer who once said to me "give me any technical challenge in the world and I will be happy, but please, please do not put me in charge of people." Andrew is not the only example of this at the extreme end of having an aversion to leadership or management roles. Like many others, Andrew had been in leadership roles early in his career and found that dealing with people and their day-to-day issues was draining all of his motivation from his day-to-day work and, worst still, it was taking him away from what he truly loved: solving problems, building things, and coding.

Andrew has made a conscious and clearly stated decision that leadership is not for him. He doesn't enjoy it and would prefer to just stick to what he is good at. To be clear, there is absolutely nothing wrong with that. In fact it is a positive. Forcing Andrew into a leadership role would only result in his team having a poor leader, Andrew being unmotivated and stressed, and the company losing one its best software architects. This does not mean that Andrew cannot lead in other ways. He can become a great mentor and teacher to other software engineers and architects. Sharing his wisdom and experience on his technical craft, but avoiding putting Andrew in a people leadership role where he is responsible for the welfare and wellbeing of his team. As a further example of the importance of this, people like Andrew with deep technical prowess can often be very influential on the culture of the organization. If Andrew becomes disenfranchised and frustrated with the state of the business, this can soon start spreading around the technical community within the company. You need people like Andrew to remain very happy and become a role model of team behaviors.

Another group of people are the ones that become disillusioned about leadership, you may have come across people like this in your career as well. Prior to going into a leadership role, they had formed a picture in their mind about what it meant to be "the boss" and then get disheartened when reality does not match their preconceived view. One of my coaching clients, during our first few sessions, was a clear example of this. Julia would often make comments like "I am telling them what they need to do and they just don't do it, they resist and challenge everything I say, and they just don't respect me," or "I am the boss; why don't they do what I say?" Julia had formed a view that a boss was someone to be respected at all times, never challenged, and the role was to direct the work of everyone. Reality is very different to this. Julia came into her first leadership role seeking "power" and discovered that this power was not what she thought it was.

After several coaching sessions Julia did find her passion for leadership. She came to the realization that there was something more deeply rewarding and satisfying by inspiring people into action because they "wanted to do it" rather than because they were "told to do it."

As you transition to and from different leadership positions in your career, it is important to check in with yourself and make sure your picture of what it means to be a leader is clear, ensure that you do indeed want to be a leader, and have an understanding of why you want to be a leader.

Test your idea of what it means to be a leader

Consider the role models that you have had in your career. Have you had people that were true leaders? Have you had people that were just on a "power trip" and liked to be "the boss" and tell people what to do?

As you transition in leadership, do you have a clear picture of what this means? Do you have realistic expectations of what will be expected of you as a leader? Are you ready to "reset" your viewpoint if there is a mismatch.

What are your motivations?

Take the time now to answer some key questions on why you want to become a leader. Is it simply because it is expected of you? Have you been tapped on the shoulder and asked to step into a leadership role? Or is this something that you are truly passionate about?

Consider your deepest motivations for becoming a leader. Do they match your own personal vision and your personal why?

How would you like your team to describe you as a leader? What are the words that they would use? How do you want to be seen by your team? How do you want to be seen by your colleagues? How do you want to be seen by your boss? Something to keep in mind is that unless you are a Founder and CEO is that while you are now a leader of your team, you are also part of a bigger team and have a boss and peers that will have expectations of you.

If your answers are more about "I want to be the boss," or "I want to be able to tell people what to do," you may want to rethink this opportunity.

If your answers are more aligned to "I want to take care of my people," "I want to nurture their development and help them to become their best," "I want to show them every day that I care," "I want to inspire them into action because they want to do it," "I want to inspire people toward a common vision, mission, and cause" then leadership may be for you.

Putting It Into Action

To help you with the above thinking and consideration, you may wish to have a deep and meaningful discussion with a trusted friend or confidant. This could be a mentor or a leader that you admire, a close friend that knows you well, or a professional such as a certified coach to talk this through.

You may wish to pick more than one. Pick some people that know you well. People who can challenge you on your answers and give you honest and frank feedback. Pick some people that can be more objective and removed from your day-to-day life. Take the time to consider strongly whether this is for you. I do hope that you take the leap. Being a leader is one of the most rewarding career steps you can ever make, but as mentioned it is not for everyone. If you try this and discover it is not for you, there is also no shame in admitting that. This is best managed with a very open and transparent conversation with your boss. Please keep in mind, this is not a failure, just something that wasn't for you. Your boss almost certainly values you for what you bring to the table or you would never have been considered for the leadership position in the first place. Your boss will appreciate the opportunity to talk through with you some options that keep you in the organisation and keep your skills in the team, but in a different form.

Consider taking on the services of a professional and certified leadership coach to help you with making this decision and making this transition a successful one. A leadership coach can help you greatly every step along the way. This provides you with someone that understands the psychology of leadership. This includes your own mindset as well as understanding the mindset of your team. When you are having challenges (and you will have them) a coach can be invaluable in helping you navigate through them. I recommend that when seeking the services of a coach that you check their credentials. Not all coaches are equal or have the same skills and accreditation. First step would be to check that they have been certified by an accredited body like the International Coaching Federation (ICF). There are some coaching programs out there that give as little as three days of training in being a coach and then release coaches out into the wild. With ICF, even at the base level, the coach has been through 60 hours of accredited training typically delivered over months, 100 hours of practice and are trained in the psychology of transformative coaching.

The next step may be to look for a coach that specializes in your field (for example Leadership) rather than just a general coach.

If you would like support in finding a suitable coach, please do reach out to The Leadership Project at www.mickspiers.com and we will provide some recommendations for you based on your individual needs.

Moment of self-reflection

From this chapter, consider the following in your moment of self-reflection:

1. What do I believe it means to be a leader?
2. Why do I want to be a leader?
3. How do I want to be perceived by my team?
4. Is leadership truly for me?
5. Who can I engage to help me with this?

Chapter Five

How People Learn

How people learn

A key underlying principle in understanding leadership and the lessons in this book relates to the way people learn, retain knowledge, and put it into practice, and how people's learning preferences are changing over time. Developing an understanding of how people learn will have a transformative shift in how you think about leadership. Understanding how people learn helps you to influence and inspire them into action and to help them to develop as an individual. The goal here is to increase their ability to learn new knowledge, retain that knowledge, and to put it into action.

Understanding the psychology of how people learn underpins my approach to everything from coaching to conversations with team members to how we conduct meetings and workshops. It also underpins my approach to learning through self-reflection.

One representation that is often used to describe this concept is Glasser's Pyramid.

...**10%** of what we read
...**20%** of what we listen
...**30%** of what we see
...**50%** of what we see and listen
...**70%** of what we discuss
...**80%** of what we do
...**95%** of what we show

-William Glasser

There is a lot of debate over the origins of Glasser's Pyramid and derision about its "exact measurements" for each layer. However, it is designed to give a simpler representation of Glasser's deep work on Choice Theory [5] and Choice Theory in the Classroom [6]. Don't put too much credence to the percentages represented, but do take note of the principle being illustrated. Many of the people that debate over the origins of the pyramid still refer to its "truthiness" and that it seems about right.

The fundamental tenet of Glasser's Choice Theory are that human beings have five needs:

- Survival
- Love and belonging
- Power (which is most closely aligned with receiving attention and feeling that we matter)
- Fun
- Freedom (Freedom to make our own choices and, Freedom from oppression)

When Choice Theory is applied to the way people learn, this translates to a need to make up our own minds, to feel that we belong, and to have fun along the way. The element of choice is fundamental to our approach to leadership. People want to feel that they are the ones holding the steering wheel of their lives. They are the ones making choices and decisions that influence their life. They may be following you as their leader, but they have a fundamental need to feel that they made that decision to follow you and to follow decisions that you may be making that impact them. The needs of survival and for love & belonging are primal. These can lead to phenomena like social conformance where their need for survival (and tribalism) and the need for love & belonging outweigh their need to be right.

The pyramids depicts that people only retain 10 percent of what they read (acutely aware you are reading a book right now, sorry), 20 percent of what they hear (welcome to all listening to this on the audiobook), 30 percent of what they see, and 50 percent of what they see and hear. These percentages are not very high.

Whereas people will retain 70 percent of what they discuss with other people (referred to as collaborative (or social) learning, 80 percent of what they experience (or discover for) themselves, and 95 percent of what they teach to someone else!

The overall picture is that people have more transformative learning through experiential learning rather than being "taught" or "told" something.

So, throughout this book you will see these principles in practice. It underpins everything from being the last to speak to how to do performance appraisals.

If we give people the room to grow and an environment where they go through a journey of discovery for themselves, they will retain and implement new learnings and new ways of thinking far more effectively. To add further reinforcement, if we get the team to discuss key learnings together and teach each other, the level of retention just continues to grow.

The added bonus along the way is that they then truly feel empowered, enabled, and energized. They will feel that their opinions are valued, take ownership and accountability for their contributions, and will feel that they matter. In summary, you will have a team that has a learning mindset and are fully engaged in everything they do.

Having a clear understanding of how people learn and about their fundamental needs described in Glasser's Choice Theory has a profound effect on how you approach leading human beings.

Learning Preferences are changing with generations

There is a notable change happening in the world of Learning & Development that we should all be cognizant of. Learning preferences are changing generationally. There could be many reasons why this is occurring including the continued proliferation of technology and social media and changes in the way school curriculum are designed. Millennials (Gen Y) and Gen Z in particular have different learning preferences (in general) compared to the generations before them [7].

These changes include a preference for:

1. **Collaborative (or social) learning** - the key principle of collaborative learning is to get people to talk it through. The very practice of getting people to verbalize what they are learning (in their own words) has a dramatic reinforcing effect. The process of thinking, reflecting, and sharing your own view increases the retention of that new knowledge. This process takes you on a journey of self-discovery rather than just rote learning what someone else has told you. This builds ownership of the new emerging content. The collaborative or social nature also allows people to build ideas upon each other by sharing individual perspectives. In any given situation, different people will perceive different things. The sharing of these perspectives among each other results in many aha moments for the participants and makes the sum of the learning greater than the individual parts. Collaborative learning builds upon our need to make our own choices and also builds upon our need for love and belonging [5] [6].

2. **Microlearning** - the key principle of microlearning is that people can only retain a limited amount of new information at any one point. It is also true that people may soon forget that new information if they are not able to put this new knowledge into practice and to do so quickly. I am sure you can remember times in your life where you have learned something, but if you did not soon put it into practice then you would simply forget. The microlearning approach will drive us to learn a small number of new things at a time and then immediately put it into practice prior to the next new learning. In a well-structured microlearning experience each new learning will build on the one before it with a period of applied practice in between. This is similar to the science behind habit building. It is now understood that it takes, on average, 66 days to build a new habit and that you have a much higher probability of success by taking on one new habit at a time and put it into daily practice,

3. **Gamification** - the root of gamification is to have fun. Gamification can come in various forms. It can be anything from simple game play and having fun with your cohort through to competitive or social leaderboards with scoring. With the scoring approach you could be competing against others or simply competing against yourself and looking to improve your score each time. The science here is simple. If you are having fun you are substantially more likely to keep going. A great analogy here for me relates to sport. I enjoy running, but really do not enjoy treadmills (I call them dreadmills). If you put me on a dreadmill for 30 minutes, I am thinking the whole time about when it will be over. Conversely, put me on a tennis court for two hours and at the end of the session I am asking "Really? Is it over? Can't we keep going?" The only thing that keeps me going on the dreadmill is to play little games in my head as I progress. So the lesson here is if you make learning fun people will show up and will want to continue.

4. **Coaching** - The art of coaching is in the expansion of one's mind. A professionally certified coach will artfully take you on a journey of discovery. You will discover things about yourself that you had not previously considered. Uncovering things that are already there but were previously hidden. Uncovering new ways of thinking and new perspectives. This approach builds great ownership of the result and a lasting transformation of one's mindset. I strongly encourage you to consider coaching and to take on the services of an appropriately certified coach from a recognized body like the International Coaching Federation (ICF).

5. **Mentoring** - With mentoring, you are learning from the experiences of others. This is not as transformational as the coaching experience but still has its place in the world as you learn from those that have gone before you. A good mentor can help you fast track your learning experience.

6. Very interestingly, these preferences do align nicely with what we now know about the best ways for people to retain new information

as described above with Glasser's Pyramid and Choice Theory [5][6]. For example, Collaborative or social learning encourages you to talk about your new learning with other people (the 70 percent mark of the pyramid). Microlearning encourages you to quickly put learning into practice that is similar to "experiencing it for yourself" (the 80 percent mark of the pyramid). Coaching embraces techniques that allow self-discovery (the 95 percent mark of the pyramid).

A moment of self-reflection

Take a moment now to stop, think, and reflect on your own learning experiences and preferences:

1. How do you prefer to learn?
2. Are you a visual person?
3. Do you prefer to hear?
4. Do you prefer to read?
5. Do you enjoy collaborative learning?
6. Are you more inclined to microlearning?
7. Think about the most transformative or life-changing lessons you have learned in your life. How did you come to learn those things?
8. Was it a journey of self-discovery or was it something that another person taught you?
9. Consider how you could apply this yourself as a leader. If you are looking to teach others, what approaches will you take to achieve maximum effect, retention, and application?

Chapter Six

Culture

What is Culture?

"Culture eats strategy for breakfast."

"Cultural fit is more important that technical skills."

You may have heard statements like this before. The importance of culture in business is becoming increasingly more understood, acknowledged, and accepted.

The majority of us would agree that culture is critical to the success of any business or organization but it does also raise some interesting questions:

1. What is culture?
2. Why is culture so important?
3. What are some of the pitfalls of focusing on culture alone?
4. How do you measure it?

These are all complicated topics in their own right, and we will just scratch the surface in this book.

What is Culture?

The definition of culture is the *ideas, customs, and social behavior of a particular group of people or society.*

This includes elements such as beliefs, laws, and habits of a collective group of people and could be described as their *"way of life."*

Culture becomes a reflection of your organization's values and beliefs (stated or unstated). Your individual, team, or organizational values can be described as "what you do when no one is looking?"

Over time, it becomes an ingrained pattern of behavior and attitudes of that group of people and the individuals within.

It is important to understand that your culture is not what you say it is by putting some plaque on the wall or some statement in the annual report, your culture is the way people live and work in your organization.

One key aspect of culture is the pressure test. What will be the default behavior of the team under periods of great pressure or simply when things do not go perfectly to plan. Either with pressing deadlines or when the organization feels like they are fighting for their survival—what will be the behaviour at that moment. Will people rally around and support each other, dig in and fight? Will they start leaving in droves because they no longer (or never did) believe in the vision and mission? Will they start blaming each other or covering their own backsides?

If you can understand these things, you are going a long way to understand the underlying culture of your team and your organization. It is important to note that the culture of your team may not be identical to the culture of the broader organization you are all in.

To understand the full power of culture, it is often referenced that culture will outlive the members of the group and will persist even under periods of turnover of group members, or in the case of a company, the employees.

This is particularly true with regard to learned behavior and corporate knowledge.

The famous, and perhaps unethical, story called "The Five Monkeys Experiment" illustrates the power of group or herd learned behavior. Please note I am using the word "story" here and not "study" as my research did not find that this experiment ever actually happened. The storytelling is compelling so I will share it here. Please read on for examples of experiments that I can confirm did occur. The short version is that five monkeys were put in a cage, and at the top of the cage a bunch of bananas were placed there for the monkeys to see. As one of the monkeys climbed up to reach for the bananas, the monkey was hosed down with cold water and so were the rest of the monkeys in the confinement. This went on for several days. The monkeys then learned what was going on and started to hold back any monkey that would reach for the bananas as they did not want to get cold and wet. Once the research team had decided that a point of collective knowledge had been achieved they proceeded to replace the monkeys one by one. As each new monkey was introduced to the group, their natural tendency was to reach for the bananas when introduced and the rest of the group would aggressively hold them back so that the group would not be hosed.

The most compelling part of the story is that this learned behavior continued on well past the point where all of the monkeys had been replaced and no monkey had any personal memory of the hosing and cold water. This story illustrates that culture can persist well beyond the tenure of your existing team and becomes very much ingrained in your organization.

Another (more ethical) example was a study conducted in the waiting room of an eye doctor [8]. The waiting room was full of 10 patients; nine of them were actors and one was the initial subject of the experiment. Every few minutes there was an audible beep played in the waiting room, and the nine actors would proceed to stand up for a moment and then sit back down. Within three of these beeps, the unsuspecting subject was standing up and joining in with the crowd, not wanting to stand out or be different.

The most interesting part is what happened as the experiment continued. One by one, the actors left the room to go in for their fictitious eye appointments. Eventually, the room was whittled down to just the subject. So what do you think happened at the next beep? That's right, even after all of her peers had left the room, at the next beep the subject still stood up with no understanding at all as to why she was doing it.

For the next phase of the experiment, new unsuspecting subjects were brought into the room one by one. At the next beep, the original subject stood up. The new subject noticed but didn't initially react. On the second beep it got the better of him and he asked Subject 1 why she was standing. Her simple answer was "I don't know, everyone else was doing it." From the next beep on, Subject 2 was now standing as well, completely oblivious to any rhyme or reason to it. As each new subject was introduced into the room, the pattern just kept repeating itself: initial puzzled looks, then conformance. Even one subject who resisted with a look of disdain for a period of three beeps also eventually started standing up on cue.

A key lesson here is to not underestimate the power of social conformance. Glasser's Choice Theory [5] tells us that people want to make their own decisions about their life. Glasser also explains that people have 5 needs with the first 2 being survival and love & belonging. Social conformance drives us to do unexpected things. This can be best explained as people making a choice that their need for survival (and a form of tribalism) and their need for love & belonging can outweigh their need to be right.

This was also demonstrated through the infamous Asch experiment [9]. The Asch experiment involves subjects being asked to answer simple questions in a group environment. Similar to the experiment above there are 5 co-conspirators (actors) to the experiment and one subject. The 5 actors would randomly choose a question to answer with an obviously incorrect answer. The study showed that the subject would go along with that wrong answer giving prove that people's need for belonging can be strong than their need to be right.

What does this mean for your company or organization?

Setting the culture of your team, business, or organization is critical. It sets the scene for learned and instinctive behaviors and norms of the group.

It can become either a virtuous cycle or a spiral depending on how this is managed. Consider in your own business and team; what are those learned behaviors? Are they adding value or holding you back?

One of the most dangerous phrases that can hold any organization back from achieving great heights of innovation and performance is "That is the way we have always done it." As you can see from the experiment above, this can outlive any living memory as to why things are done that way. If you are continuing to do things a certain way but no one can really remember why it is done that way you are almost certainly not maximizing your impact. There needs to be a good understanding of *why* something is done before you can optimize the approach on how it is done.

How is culture established?

The leaders and leadership of the organization have the most critical role in setting the culture. This can be challenging and daunting. The most powerful questions you can ask to understand and to shift the culture in your business are the following:

1. **What behaviors are rewarded / celebrated?** – People are finely tuned in and watching what behaviors receive praise and other rewards. For example, if they see people that work long hours in crisis mode are put on a pedestal they will learn that behavior.

2. **What behaviors are tolerated?** – Tolerated behavior is a form of implicit acceptance. This is key when it comes to inappropriate behavior or behavior that is incongruent with your values. If people witness a team member with questionable behaviors "getting away with it" they will learn this too. In this case it generally triggers a binary reaction. They either start mimicking those behaviors too, or they will be outraged with the behavior and be shocked that it wasn't addressed. In the latter case, they may even decide to look for the door and leave the business. This is particularly true if that questionable behavior was contrary to their personal values and beliefs of right and wrong

3. **What behaviors are <u>not</u> tolerated?** – This can be a positive reinforcement or a negative spiral. I will give 2 examples here. The converse of the example above (in tolerated behavior) is when inappropriate behavior is quickly and effectively addressed. People will see that this behavior is not acceptable. They will learn from this and they will appreciate the values and culture of the company. The negative side is where positive and healthy behaviors are not tolerated. If you want to have psychological safety in your teams, a healthy environment where people aren't scared to speak up, you need to ensure that people are not chastised or punished for "challenging the boss" or other similar behaviors. If this is not

tolerated people will soon learn not to speak their mind to the detriment of the business in the long-run.

Why is Culture Important?

The importance of culture cannot be overstated. Your culture becomes a determining factor in how the world sees your organization including customers and prospective employees. It will influence the type of people you attract to the business and which people thrive in that environment. Is your culture "win at all costs," "customer centric," "ethically driven," "altruistic," "people focused"?

There is not necessarily a right or wrong answer to any of that, but it is important to know.

It is critical that culture, behavior, and actions are consistent with the stated values of the company and that of the leaders in your organization. When there is a mismatch between these there is an erosion of trust and messages from senior management start sounding like rhetoric. If you say you are "people-first," make sure your decisions and actions match your statements.

One way of understanding the importance of consistency is to consider what happens when it is not there. A good way to destroy trust and de-motivate your team is to not take action when a team member's behavior is inconsistent with the culture and values of the team. Inaction will serve as an implicit endorsement that this behavior is acceptable. That behavior will then continue, or worse still increase and all that see this will be demoralized and start looking for the door.

Best is the Standard

An organization that I have recently had the deep pleasure of working with shows a good illustration of a great approach to setting the culture of the business. During the writing and production of this book, I have been working with the Self-Publishing School. The Founder, Chandler Bolt, shows a maturity well beyond his youth. From everything I see from the outside he has established an amazing culture that will become the legacy of that company for years to come.

This culture is a balance of people that genuinely believe in the vision of the organization, genuinely care for their customers, and a belief in accountability and performance.

The vision is very clear that they help people to write books so they can grow their impact, income, and business.

The focus for the team is also made very clear to them. In everything they do they need to focus on either gaining new customers or absolutely delighting their existing customers.

Their mantra is that "Best is the Standard." This does not mean that they need to be the best at everything they do. It means that each team member strives to do *their* best work every day. They will ask themselves and each other "Is this **your** best work?" which drives a culture of performance and continuous improvement at a team and individual level.

Accountability is also driven through clear performance indicators. Every performance indicator in the business has a single owner and every person in the business knows how their own KPI contributes to the overall success of the business.

When can a focus on culture become a bad thing?

A challenging question that then arises, if culture is so critical then when can that be a bad thing? The first issue is when the focus on culture comes at the expense of diversity. There is a potential trap of thinking that cultural fit means just employing "like-minded" people. Culture should be based on values and beliefs and not based on just having people with common backgrounds. Anybody that has spent any period of time with me will know the high value I place on diversity of thought and on an inclusive workplace. Be very careful to ensure that the strive for "cultural fit" does not become a blind spot for a lack of diversity. This can be done by taking a step back and ensuring that your focus on "cultural fit" is not driving you to only employ people that look, think, and act like you.

Going a step further, you also need to ensure that a focus on culture does not become an issue for inclusion. To create an inclusive workplace and team, we need to ensure that everyone feels that they belong and that no one feels excluded. True inclusion would create an environment where people feel welcome and valued for their true authentic self. Inclusion is not, and should not be, assimilation. Your role as a leader is to create a wonderful culture and environment where everyone feels proud of their heritage, background, and experiences and feel that they belong to an amazing group of people working toward a common vision and purpose and with shared values and beliefs. This can be achieved by providing a platform for people to share their story. You want to achieve an environment where there is no discrimination, bias, or prejudice and where people celebrate their heritage and uniqueness.

The next issue can be a lack of accountability. In high-performance teams every person has their role to play and all other team members are relying on them. We do need to be careful that we do not diminish accountability and excuse it away because someone is a great "cultural fit."

So, how might you bring these things together? How might you balance a priority on culture while ensuring you do not lose any commitment to diversity, inclusion, and accountability? The simple answer is to ensure that these things that you value are part of the culture. Make valuing and celebrating diversity and creating an inclusive workplace one of the stated values and beliefs of the team. You can then collectively hold each other to account for your performance against these values and living by these beliefs.

How do we measure culture?

This brings us to how we might measure culture in our teams and in our leaders.

There is definitely more than one way to measure the culture of a business and to understand whether it aligns with the culture that the organization is trying to build.

A key first step in any approach would be to be very clear and upfront about the values and beliefs of the business and to make sure that this is reinforced on a frequent basis in all parts of the organization. As a leader in the business it is your responsibility to seek out and find the stated values and beliefs of the organization and reinforce them in your team. This will be on top of being clear about your own values and beliefs and how these align with the organization and what your team does.

Some key approaches that many organization take to measure culture include:

1. Conducting staff attitudinal surveys

2. Asking your customers their perception of your culture

3. Building values, beliefs, and culture into the performance appraisal system

You should proactively seek out the results of these surveys so that you have a clear understanding of the lay of the land in the organization and in your team.

Staff and customer surveys can take on a myriad of forms from being very formal and conducted by independent organizations that specialize in this field through to very informal and open approaches with your staff and your customers.

A key way to ensure the importance of culture is well ingrained in the organization and your team is to build it into the ratings of individuals and give it equal weighting alongside accountability for performance and results.

For this to be effective the first step is to ensure that the company's expectations of culture are well understood and people are aware that it is going to be measured.

I recently had the pleasure and honor of interviewing Sulin Lau of Grab for The Leadership Project Podcast [10], and she graciously shared with us Grab's approach to measuring culture in their staff.

Grab set clear guidance for their staff and the culture of the organization around 4 Hs: Heart, Hunger, Honor, and Humility. They provide team members and team leaders with guidance on what it means to live by these values.

Heart is about taking care of your team and taking a genuine interest in their wellbeing and personal development.

Hunger is having the desire to continuously strive for greatness and push yourself and your team to greater levels of performance and success.

Honor can be simply put as saying what you are going to do and then delivering on that promise. Honor is also about staying true and consistent to your stated values and beliefs.

Humility is about being humble but also goes deeper than that. It encompasses having intellectual humility and curiosity and understanding that you do not have all of the answers. You will never learn anything new if you already think you know it all. Without intellectual humility you will shut yourself off to new ideas and innovations that could be game-changers for you and your team.

This is then backed up and reinforced by the performance management process giving a 50:50 weighting between business outcomes and living by the 4Hs.

This is not the only way to measure culture or leadership, but I do indeed like the clarity and focus they have achieved in this approach.

A moment of self-reflection

Take a moment now to stop, reflect, and think on the following questions:

1. How does your company or organization set and measure culture?
2. What actions do you take to reinforce that in your teams?
3. What behaviors are rewarded and celebrated?
4. What behaviors are tolerated (turning a blind eye)?
5. What behaviors are not tolerated (good and bad)?
6. What do you think your customers, stakeholders, and people outside the organization would say is your culture (stated or unstated)?
7. What do you think the people inside your organization would say is your culture (stated or unstated)?
8. How would your culture stand up to the pressure test? When pressure is at its highest, does the culture withstand that pressure or does some other underlying culture emerge?

If you would like to hear more from Sulin Lau and her own personal journey moving from individual contributor to inspirational leader, please do take a listen to her two-part interview series on The Leadership Project Podcast.

Chapter Seven

Mistakes All New Leaders Make

What are the most common mistakes all new leaders make?

There are certain mistakes that nearly all leaders make early in their leadership career.

For some, these will come very early, for others the onset will be later and/or the self-realization of the mistake will take time to emerge.

Mistake #1 - Being the answer to every question

A key mistake most leaders make is becoming the answer to every single question their team raises. This generally comes from a good place in the leader's heart. They want to be supportive and they want to show their value. Where the issue arises is that this does not allow the team the opportunity to learn and grow and think for themselves.

Instead of answering every question immediately, consider pausing and offering a growth opportunity to your team instead. This can be challenging if you already know the answer, but remember this is not about you, it is about them. Rather than give an immediate answer, try asking some exploratory questions back to them. These questions could be for more context and definitely should be to ask them about their opinion on the topic at hand.

This has benefits on many levels. By listening to the team you are showing that you value their opinion— "Oh, wait, the boss really wants to know what I think." It provides opportunities to explore additional options that you may not have considered. It provides you with the opportunity to test your team members' awareness (self-awareness and situational awareness). It teaches your team members to be able to think for themselves, and ultimately will result in your team becoming more self-sufficient so they are not always reliant on you for answers.

So, as mentioned, a smarter approach is always to ask more questions than you give answers. You may need to subtly coach or guide your team to the answer and the way forward, but do so in a way that is a learning experience based on "self-discovery" rather than just teaching them what to do. If you just give someone the answer they will remember it for a day, but if they discover the answer themselves they will remember it forever.

Mistake #2 - "Doing" too much

It is a very common mistake to see newly appointed leaders try to "do" too much. If they have been promoted from within the ranks they will often continue to do large chunks of their old role as well as taking on their new responsibilities. This can be veiled in thinking they are "leading from the front" or "leading by example" and the leader ends up working incredibly long hours with increasing pressure weighing down on their shoulders. This can also be gilded with the thought they are the best person for every job. The best person to give a presentation, the best person to attend a meeting, the best person to develop a new deliverable, etc, etc.

Beyond the inevitable burnout risk that comes with this, the biggest issue is that it robs their team of development opportunities for their own and the opportunity to shine.

I would encourage you to try "doing" less and give more opportunities to people around you. This, in turn, gives you many benefits. It shows the team that you trust them. It gives empowerment and drives deep engagement and ownership. It provides you with the chance to see them in action and see if you have hidden talents in your team. It provides you with a great opportunity to search for who could be candidates to be your successor.

Mistake #3 - Wanting to be the smartest in the room

As a leader, you will soon be engaged in leadership-team meetings with your peers all reporting into your boss. A common mistake that many leaders make is to try to "prove" themselves or prove their value in front of their boss and in front of their peers.

It is critically important that you do contribute to those conversations and be active in that leadership team, but it is not a competition to see who can be the smartest in the room.

Avoid any kind of point scoring mentality, be collegiate and supportive with your peers and your boss, and contribute constructively. This will not go unnoticed by your boss and the rest of the team.

This does include having the courage to ask questions if you are uncertain about a topic or if you have concerns, but always do so in a constructive and respectful manner.

Many of the same leadership values and attributes that you need to demonstrate with your own team apply when you are at the leadership table. This includes truly listening to your peers and to demonstrate that you are present and in the moment. A key point to remember is that listening is not the same as waiting for your turn to speak.

Mistake #4 - Being Close Minded to Alternate Approaches.

Please always remember that different is not necessarily wrong. Wrong is wrong, but different is not always wrong.

There is always more than one way to solve any problem or do any task. If one of your team members takes a different approach to the way you would have done the same task, rather than immediately correct them, keep an open mind and assess their approach on its own merits. Does it achieve the same objective in a different way? Does it achieve the outcome in an even better way? Does it just require some fine tuning? There is a great power in having the team member feel empowered and take ownership of their own method to achieve the outcome that is far richer than you just showing them what and how you would have done it.

This issue is particularly prevalent if you have just been promoted from the very role they are performing. If you are the previous incumbent of their role or doing that job as part of the team, you are almost certainly going to have your own (potentially strong) views on the way this job is done. You do need to be there to support and guide, but they will learn so much more, be more creative, and will take more ownership if you allow them the license to discover the role for themselves.

Mistake #5 - Correcting Mistakes Yourself

The tendency to want to correct mistakes myself is something I personally had issues with in the past and still comes up from time to time. I am sure you have all experienced something like this before, either on the receiving end or as the reviewer of other people's work. The scenario is that someone has written a document, report, or proposal and you are reviewing it for approval. As you review the work you start to find a number of mistakes in approach, content, or grammar. The expedient approach and temptation may lead you to just fix it yourself. This leads to famous, but unhelpful, statements like "Don't worry I will just do it myself" or "If you want something done right, do it yourself." These are both very limiting statements that make me cringe when I hear them.

Consider what happens if this is your default approach. Each time you do this it disenfranchises or disempowers the original author. It is also a lost opportunity for learning and development for that person. Worst still it sets a pattern of behavior. The pattern will continue to repeat itself. The same mistakes will be recreated time and time again. Beyond that, the person may even come to rely on this. "No problem, I will just quickly put something together and the boss will fix it (or correct it)," removing all care and accountability.

There are moments in time that you may need to just correct the work and get on with it, for example a pressing and immovable deadline. However, this should be the exception not the rule.

When these situations arise, and they will, the best approach is to turn everything into a learning opportunity based on self-discovery for the author. At a minimum, spend the time with that author to explain corrections needed. Better still, ask them questions like "How do you think we could improve this statement?" Or "Can you think of ways that this phrase could be misinterpreted by the reader?" These types of questions will build far more memorable lessons and ownership on your team member's behalf.

Some other factors that creep in here are whether you are imposing your own personal standards on others, particularly with regard to perfectionism. A lesson, in many contexts, that can be difficult to learn is the concept that "done is better than perfect." There are times where just getting the job done is more important than having a perfect solution or product and there can be diminishing returns from the extra time put into the final stages of that work. Clearly, this one needs to be taken on a case-by-case basis.

Mistake #6 - Expressing your opinion too early

Your team members will always be looking to please you. This leads to them looking for signals from you about what you would like and which direction to go. First-time leaders will often default to "telling" rather than "engaging" their teams. When they realize this is not working, they will graduate to statements like "This is what I think, but I am interested in your views, so what do you think?" By taking this approach, you have already planted the seed in their mind about your preferences and you will have already closed down ideation on new ideas. Staff members that may be just looking to please you will in turn just rephrase your statement to show support of you rather than really thinking critically about the topic at hand.

This can be expanded to all kinds of situations. I have coached a number of new leaders that come to me with the presenting issue of "I've told my team what to do and they just aren't doing (or getting) it." In almost any situation, you will get a much greater level of engagement if you start with a "blank sheet of paper" or a "clean whiteboard" and brainstorm through the issue at hand. You may need to set the scene at the start of the meeting, but even then don't overdo this. At the start of the meeting you need to test the team's awareness of the topic. Good examples could include "Today we are going to discuss our xxx process; let's start with what we feel is working and not working with the current approach." Building that awareness is crucial if you plan to motivate people to realize that some level of change is necessary. After establishing awareness of how the current process works (and where it doesn't work), you can then start ideating some possible solutions. Once again being very careful not to express your own opinion too early.

You can build on this further by asking more probing questions like "What is not being said that needs to be said?" In doing so, giving people the license and psychologically safe environment to truly express what is on their mind.

At the end of the meeting, it is critically important to summarise the top three to five outcomes of the discussion. There are countless examples in the world where a group of people have walked away from a meeting thinking they all know what just happened, only to discover later that there was no common understanding.

This summary is something that you can do yourself, or you could even take the step of having one of the team do the summary, thereby building further engagement. You may be even bolder and pick the person in the room that you think is most likely to be sceptical or resistant to the change and give them the pen for the summary. They will be more engaged from this, take more ownership, and will find it very difficult to argue against the summary later if they are the ones that had the pen in their hand. You will need to use some judgment and emotional intelligence to decide when to and when *not* to do this.

Mistake #7 - Avoiding challenging conversations

This can stem from a number of different factors. It may be that you genuinely do not enjoy confrontation, or it could be that you are trying too hard to be liked. This has been a hard lesson to learn in my career and something that I am still working on. The realization that I have made is that most people thrive on feedback (both positive and constructive). Positive feedback is critical for reinforcing and recognizing great work and positive behaviors. By providing that positive feedback, the person feels valued and gets the clear signal to "do more" of what they are already doing. Constructive feedback is critical for awareness. The topic may well be a blind spot for the person involved, and they cannot fix what they do not know about.

I, for one, personally find that feedback is a gift, and I seek it out whenever I can. This feedback helps me to identify any of my own blind spots in my performance and helps me to empathize and understand the emotions and opinions of the people I am working with.

So, with the fact that I enjoy and appreciate feedback so much, I came to the realization that others do as well. Giving your team constructive feedback is a show of respect for them. It shows that you care about their personal and professional development. Rather than not liking you, it will actually build even more respect for you when you provide this feedback and invest in them.

Giving them positive feedback demonstrates that you "see" them and notice and appreciate what they do. Giving constructive feedback is a sign of love, respect, and care. It shows that your care for them is greater than your fear of a confronting conversation.

The other lesson that I have taken is that you should give feedback early and often. If you wait too long to give positive feedback, you may have already deteriorated the person's attitude: "I am putting in my best work here and no one even notices." There will be a high probability that, uncorrected, the issue becomes amplified. The conversation will now be even more challenging and difficult to correct because you left it too long to address. Circling back to the point above, you may have also been spending a lot of extra hours correcting work yourself, which creates an unhealthy cycle and habit.

Mistake #8 - Not knowing when to escalate and when not to

This one will take some time to learn and get your mind around. It will also be different depending on the preferences of your boss and your level in the organization and the expectations of what you should be able to manage yourself and what you would be expected to escalate.

In all situations, it would be advisable to have this conversation with your boss soon after your appointment to your new role. Ask direct questions like "What level of escalation and information would you expect from me?" "Are there topics that are particularly important to you where you will always want to be informed?" and "How do you prefer to be informed of emerging situations, issues, or problems?" Your boss should be very happy to share these with you.

There are some generalizations that will mostly stand true. Bosses have a strong preference for open and transparent communication and trust will soon be broken if you are found to be "hiding" things, thinking you can manage it yourself.

Initially err on the side of over-communicating. You will soon learn which topics your boss gets most animated and engaged in and which ones are less important to them. You will then be able to start judging which issues would require escalation, which are candidates for just informing the boss "This is going on, but I have it under control, just an FYI," and which you can comfortably manage without any need for passing through.

Moment of self-reflection

Take a moment now to reflect on these common mistakes above.

1. How many of these have you fallen into the trap of?
2. Have you seen others make similar mistakes?
3. How will you consider these learnings to avoid some of these common pitfalls?

Chapter Eight

Learning from leaders around you

Whenever I meet someone new as part of The Leadership Project, I invariably end up asking them a question about great and inspiring leaders they have had. I also ask the opposite—bosses at the other end of the scale. Ones that didn't inspire them or in many cases demoralized them.

At the virtuous end of that spectrum, I uncovered great stories and examples of leaders who were able to both attract and retain talented people with the express desire to work with them. For example, Anne Parmer (from The Leadership Project podcast episode 11[11] joined and stayed at Celerity because of the vision of Ken Quiglio, his values and leadership style, and the psychologically safe environment he provides for his team.

Unfortunately, at the other end of the spectrum, there are far too many examples of the opposite. People can often remember two or three inspirational leaders that they have worked with, but can nearly always remember a long list of managers that demotivated them or treated them poorly.

I am no exception to this, I have had some great leaders in my time that I will always look up to and remember them with great love. Many are mentioned specifically in this book. However, I also can list a number of managers that I will never forget for the wrong reasons and that includes three examples where I left organizations because the situation had become untenable with my personal values.

A common thread of my story and of all of the stories that people shared with me was *emotion*.

As Maya Angelou is famously attributed as saying, "People may not remember what you did or what you said, but they will always remember how you made them feel."

This is true in every aspect of life, and leaders are no exception to this.

Collect Lessons from all leaders

It is important to bring these experiences into actionable practice. Capture lessons learned from all leaders you have worked with past, present, and future. Create your own knowledge base of what worked, what didn't work, and how the actions of these leaders and managers made you feel.

Keep an eye out to the left and right of you and see the emotional reactions of your peers to those same triggers. Do not underestimate the importance of this. No two people on this planet are the same. The leadership practice that inspires and motivates you may not have the same impact on the person to your right or left. The key here is to be observant.

Don't limit yourself to your immediate leader or manager. Look up, down, and sideways in your organization, and identify those key practices and actions.

Look outside your organization too. You could come into direct contact with customers, partners, and suppliers. It could be the team leader at your local coffee shop, or it could be leaders of companies or brands that you admire.

Look across the spectrum

These leadership lessons will sit across a spectrum from inspirational to demoralizing. Many leaders will sit somewhere on that spectrum, where they have some admirable traits and some approaches that don't work well for you.

The key here is to look for both in all leaders and write them down. Write down the action or approach, write down whether it was positive or negative, write down how it made you feel, and write down the lesson you are taking away from it.

You may wish to capture these notes in your self-reflection journal. You can download a copy of The Leadership Project Self-Reflection Journal at www.mickspiers.com

The process of writing these details down, including the emotions you felt, enables you to identify any patterns of leadership practices you admire and would like to emulate and wish ones you want to avoid repeating.

Different is not necessarily wrong

Keep an open mind throughout this process and remember that different is not necessarily *wrong*. As we strive to challenge the status quo, it may well be that *different* and innovative approaches are what we need.

What does not work for you may work perfectly fine for those around you (and vice versa).

There is always more than one way to achieve a certain outcome or result, and leadership practices are no exception to that.

Time is also a factor here. Different leaders have different levels of urgency for a given task. One leader may be very happy to give their team a lot of time and a lot of space to get through a specific task, and they may have good reasons for doing so. The more space and time you give the team, the more they may learn.

My Amalgam Leader

When I pay attention to inspirational leaders I have had in the past, I build an amalgam of these leaders to bring together all of their virtuous traits into one.

An amalgam leader is the sum of all of the virtuous traits of the inspirational leaders I have had in the past. There is no single leader that is perfect at everything. So the amalgam leader is coupling together the positives from a range of leaders rather than just admiring one specific leader.

I encourage you to build your own amalgam leader. We have provided a template for doing so in The Leadership Project Self-Reflection Journal available for download at www.mickspiers.com

My amalgam leader would be a combination of the following amazing and inspirational leaders:

- Chris Jenkins - "the relatable one" with executive presence and Mana, clear vision coupled with the ability to relate to anyone from the Prime Minister through to a welder in the shipyard.
- Millar Crawford - "the storyteller" that leads by example, researches new topics deeply, has exceptional storytelling, and the ability to understand the complex and navigate through tricky waters.
- Laurent Eskenazi - "the backer" with the ability to empower you and back your judgment when you put forward a well-thought-through plan. Master of the "No Blame Culture."
- Matt Cole - "the visionary" with exceptional presentation and communication skills to inspire people into action around that vision. This also extended to a strong ability to project that vision through the brand of the company.
- Jeff Lowinger - "the accountable" - exceptional at driving a new level of accountability. The ability to look at the present and the future and not blame things on the past. You have to accept the cards you are dealt and make the best possible use of all levers at your disposal rather than use excuses about the past. Exceptional at knowing when to step in and protect the team in front of the board and when to let the team sweat a little. Not easy to describe this great balance but essentially he ensures the team gets great praise for their successes and steps in and takes accountability when things don't go perfectly according to plan. Jeff is also a great advocate for diversity, equity, and inclusion through being an ally, standing up for what's right, speaking out against things that are not right, and making sure this is through positive action not just rhetoric and sound bites.
- Major General David Hurley - "matter" builds connection and makes you always feel that you matter. General Hurley, well before becoming Governor-General of Australia, had an exceptional ability for remembering who you are, what you are working on, and what is going on in your personal life.

- Tom Walker - "the summarizer" with the ability to filter, sift through the details, and summarize what is most important. Tom is exceptional at "being the last to speak." He can sit through a long(ish) meeting, giving all team members the psychologically safe environment to voice their opinions, keeping an open mind at all times. Then, as the meeting would draw to a close, he had an uncanny ability to summarize what was most important from the meeting. This would inevitably result in everyone in the meeting giving knowing smiles and nods to each other as if to say "Tom is right.......again." All done in a manner such that you know that your opinion was valued along the way.

As I build this amalgam leader, I also remember all of the bad bosses (and/or bad moments) in my career where someone has made me frustrated, demotivated, or sometimes far worse. For legal reasons I will not be naming these ones specifically, but what I do is take these moments, remember what they did and how they made me feel so that I can do my best to avoid making my own team ever feel that way. For those who know me well, I will also respectfully ask that you do not try to guess who these people are. Here is a summary list:

- Perhaps one of the worst moments in my career was the executive who asked me when I was a director to fire my best team member for no apparent reason. The barrage was constant at every one-on-one meeting for many weeks in a row. They would ask/tell me "you have to fire xxxxx." After months of refusing to do so unless she gave me good reasons, I decided that my position with her was untenable and I left that job. About six months later I discovered the reason. On his very first meeting with the executive, my staff member said, "Oh, I see you have joined us from company XYZ, you must know a good friend of mine, John." Little did he know at that time, his good friend was the person who had terminated her from her previous company on performance grounds. There are so many things I took away from that experience that I almost don't know where to begin.
  - o Never ask someone to do something unless you can explain the reasons why

- o Never put your own personal motivations ahead of others
- o Never punish another for your own self-protection

- The contradictor. This is a challenging one, but I have worked for one senior executive who would give contradictory directions from one day to the next. One of the biggest issues here is that I am not certain that they were always aware that the direction was inconsistent. This would include "direction" to go and spend money on extra resources to get a job done quickly and then immediately get upset at the very same cost in the next meeting. Other examples would be to develop policies that contradict each other. The challenge here is that individually the policies would make sense, but when combined together they would be in conflict and with no guidance one should take. Some lessons to take from this one:
  - o Stop and think before giving "absolute statements" in your directions and policies
  - o Consider unintended consequences of well-meaning statements
  - o Have an open environment where people feel safe to point out to you any inconsistencies
  - o Have at least one confidant that can tell you if your directions are confusing the team
- The accidentally rhetorical question. One senior executive would hold leadership meetings where he would put people on the spot in front of the whole group and ask questions in a way that the only possible answer would be one that would please them (whether it was the right answer or not). They were not pitched as rhetorical questions, but they might as well have been. Worse still, these questions would often result in either actions that you then have to somehow try to implement or would come back later and you will be reminded of the answer you gave. This same executive would also get visibly upset when people would not speak up at meetings not realizing that they had not created an environment where people did not feel safe to speak up and where the meeting was mostly governed by fear. To avoid this, you:
  - o Ask open questions and then say nothing and listen

- o Provide a psychologically safe environment that allows people to push back and say no or give an answer that you may not like
- o Make a positive example of people when they do this so that others see that it is safe to do so

- The ever-expanding question. One senior executive would often send out a question to teams where he would expect an almost-immediate answer. So far, this is okay. However, when the answer would come back it, would immediately be responded to with three new questions, not questions that build on the answer to the original but new avenues of inquiry. Before you know it, you are spending hours just responding to questions rather than getting anything productive done. To avoid this:
  - o Break down your questions to the bare minimum needed for you to have the visibility you are looking for
  - o Do not ask questions that may unduly bring trust into doubt
  - o Ask these questions in one go rather than playing email ping pong
  - o If you foresee the topic may be complicated, call a short meeting with a clear agenda and avoid any email misunderstandings

- The Know-It-All. I have had one executive who thought he knew the answer to every question and was always ready to share it. This included being very close-minded. He would mostly enter into any meeting with a preconceived idea and would leave the meeting unmoved despite excellent debate and discussion.
  - o Simply put: always keep an open mind.

- The non-listener. This one was not a direct manager of mine, but rather a so-called peer. I have had one department head who would often come into my office unannounced and unscheduled to ask my opinion on a certain topic and would then show no signs that he was actually listening to what I was saying. Another one with preconceived ideas that were impossible to shift. The very last meeting I took with that individual resulted in me saying, "Look, you are clearly not listening to a word I am saying, so this meeting is over." I stood up and left and walked down the hallway only to realize I had left my own office. I can laugh at the fact that I left my own office, but that does not negate that this so-called peer did not make me feel valued every time he was clearly not listening. To avoid anything of this nature:

- o Practice active and deep listening every day
- o Your objective in any communication or meeting should never be a one way broadcast of your own agenda or message
- o Treat every conversation with respect and show the other person that you value their opinion and that they matter

- Rhetoric and Values. Another very sour note would be the executive that would consistently act in direct opposition to his publicly stated values and beliefs. Standing up in front of Town Hall meetings to state the values of the company and then go immediately to his next meeting and start acting in the exact opposite manner.I have three mechanisms in place to avoid this:
  - o I openly declare my values and beliefs and empower my team to call me on it if they see any behaviors are inconsistent
  - o I have these values and beliefs printed on my wall in my office as a daily reminder
  - o A practice I have learned from Brendan Bouchard of GrowthDay is to have daily alarms set in my phone with labels that remind me of the person I am and strive to be

- The "It's not me, it's you" leader. I do not want to be too specific here or it will be too obvious who I am talking about. I have had one leader in the past who genuinely thought that they were the best at everything they did. "I tell you something, I am the most xxxxxx there is." "Why can't you all be more like me." "I am not the choke point here." etc, etc. This leader would often let personal pride get in the way of taking any accountability or responsibility for the performance of the business and had almost no self-awareness of his role in setting the culture and performance of the broader team. This same leader would then get frustrated with people who would not speak up at meetings and that employee engagement scores were going backward under his leadership. To have your radar tuned for this one:

o   Practice vulnerability

o   Practice humility

o   Have people around you that will hold you accountable if you are not practicing vulnerability and humility

- The "shoot the messenger" leader. We discuss throughout this book the need to create a psychologically safe environment where people feel they can openly voice their opinions and thoughts. I have had a number of leaders that have done the exact opposite. One leader in particular, when confronted with a challenging viewpoint or bad news would do one of three things:

  o   Get defensive (see "It's not me, it's you" above)

  o   Hit the ball straight back to the questioner as hard and fast as possible (blame them)

  o   Give the questioner a barrage of actions in reward for speaking their mind.

  o   I am sure that you can quickly guess what would subsequently happen in the culture of that company. To avoid this, you must implement a blame-free culture. People will very quickly stop telling you things if you overreact to everything they say.

  o   To quote Tim McClure, "The biggest concern of any organization should be when their most passionate people become quiet," and this is exactly what happened in this business.

The most important message to take away from all of the above is that I learned valuable lessons from every one of these leaders and these experiences (the positive and the negative). To quote John C Maxwell, "Sometimes you win, sometimes you learn." You will almost certainly come across some horrendous managers and bosses in your career, and I hope that these experiences are not too traumatic for you. Regardless of what happens, to make the most of the situation, the best thing you can do is put it all down to education and learning.

Putting It Into Action

Adopt a growth mindset where you are continuously looking to learn, improve, and adapt. Collect and apply a selection of lessons from various leaders you have observed. In doing so, you will become an amazing and inspiring leader yourself.

You will become the leader that other leaders aspire to be like. People will want to come and work with you and they will want to stay.

Others are learning from you

In the same way that you are learning from other leaders, be very aware that others are watching and learning from you.

As a father of two beautiful boys, I have always enjoyed watching Henry and Thomas as they discover new things for the very first time. An amazing sequence almost invariably happens, and I believe most parents will recognize this.

On the first discovery of something new, Henry and Thomas will always take a sideways glance at someone they trust (e.g. parents, grandparents) as if to ask "Is this okay?"

At that very moment they are looking for signals, verbal or body language, as to what they should make of this new thing or experience. It could be anything from a new food, a new experience, to being passed to a relative or family friend that they don't recognize.

The reaction of the parent at that fleeting moment will have a great impact on what happens next. Positive reinforcement will usually lead to a positive experience, any look of fear or nerves will have the opposite effect.

A great illustration of this is the first swimming lesson. If a parent shows excitement and joy, the child will typically quickly learn to love the water. Conversely, any fear or concern on the face of the parent will result in a fear of water. A fear that may take a very long time to reverse.

Cognitively, this process is called reflective learning.

So, what does this have to do with leadership? Well, this phenomenon never quite goes away. It evolves over time, but people continue to look for signals from someone they trust (or someone they are seeking the approval of) whenever they experience something new. In the schoolyard this will become their peers, and in the workplace it will be the leaders.

"With great power comes great responsibility." - Uncle Ben (from Spiderman - Stan Lee)

While I do not like the negative connotations of the word power or the power struggles that happen in many companies, it is important to acknowledge the power that leaders can have and to ensure that power is used responsibly. The power to inspire people into action is something to be admired but needs to be taken with due care to ensure those actions are virtuous and to avoid unintended outcomes.

Always remember that people are looking for signals from you, particularly with regards to something new.

The best signal you could give them is that it is completely okay for them to form their own view and to provide a psychologically safe environment for them to express their opinion.

You need to be careful of the signals you are sending. Make sure they are consistent with your values, and make sure they are not leading to unintended outcomes.

Moment of self-reflection

Take a moment to stop, think, and reflect now.

1. Who are all of the leaders you have worked with?
2. Did they inspire you and the people around you?
3. Did they demoralize you and the people you work with?
4. What were their most admirable traits and actions?
5. What were their least?
6. How did they make you feel?
7. How will you put these lessons into your own leadership style?
8. If someone else was filling out these about your own leadership style, how would you rate?
9. What does your amalgam leader look like? Take the time to draw it up. Who are those leaders you want to learn positive attributes from and how would you build an amalgam leader from them?
10. When faced with something new:
11. Do your staff look to you for a signal?
12. What signals are you sending?
13. Are you providing a psychologically safe environment that allows them to express their views openly?
14. Do you ever have unintended outcomes from interpretation of those signals?

Chapter Nine

Leadership Attributes

What others look for in great leaders

One of the greatest benefits of working on The Leadership Project and The Leadership Project podcast is to survey and listen to a broad set of views about what good and great leadership looks like.

I have also been collecting over time my own personal views about leaders that I admire and that inspire me.

This has enabled me to develop a list of attributes that people look for in great leaders and the same common list comes up on a frequent basis.

An interesting point is that most of the answers relate to emotions and feelings rather than rational or tangible things.

Making people feel valued and they matter

The number one response in each survey conducted and a frequent response in all podcast interviews has been that great and inspiring leaders make their team members feel valued and feel that they matter.

This includes giving people a platform to find and share their voice and to deeply listen and demonstrate that you have listened and value their contribution and opinions.

It means taking the time to acknowledge contributions and successes in the team (individually and collectively). There is almost nothing worse than when someone works their butt off to complete a task or a report and you cannot tell if your boss even noticed or read the report.

This also includes taking the time to build a genuine connection with your team members individually. Take an interest in them personally. Remember things about them that they have previously told you about. Write handwritten notes of thanks, care and support for them. Show support and care for them when they are having a tough time, for example when they or a family member are unwell.

Take the time to understand their personal preferences and then make sure that any reward or recognition that you give them is in line with those preferences.

Trust

The number two factor in our surveys has been Trust. Trust is a two-way thing. The most common answer is that their boss trusts them and demonstrates that trust through their actions. Conversely, that the boss does not show any behavior that brings that trust into question.

One of the key drivers in building trust is to demonstrate that you trust your team and every team member. This will create a reciprocity of trust between you.

To build and maintain trust over time is to ensure that your actions are always in alignment with your stated values and beliefs.

Authenticity

An attribute that is raised with increasing frequency is that of authenticity. People crave a boss that brings their authentic self every day. Someone that is themselves and does not try to be something else. This then extrapolates to providing an environment where people can also be their authentic self and to be respected for that.

Vision, Purpose and Meaning

Another attribute highly sought after is a leader who has clarity around their own personal vision and the vision for their organization or team. These leaders are typically able to clearly articulate the purpose, positive impact and provide meaning to what the team does. That is, the *impact* of what you do, not what you do.

These leaders will have a great ability to attract and retain team members that have similar purpose. All people want to work for an organization and have a job where they can clearly see the purpose and meaning of what they do. Where they feel valued and that what they do matters. This has always been the case; however, it is becoming increasingly clear that with generational changes that this is now more important than ever. There could be a number of driving factors behind this, but Gen X, Gen Y, and Gen Z will often prioritize purpose and meaning over other attributes of a job and will leave organizations where that meaning is not evident. This also extends to corporate social responsibility. They will look to work for companies with a social conscience. Companies that are doing the right thing with regard to social issues including diversity, equity, inclusion, discrimination, and the environment. They will also leave companies if they find that these social issues are not being respected or valued in the actions of the organization.

Values and Beliefs (Consistency)

People seek to work for leaders who communicate openly about the values and beliefs that are most important to them. Critically, their behavior is then consistent with these stated values and beliefs at all times. A great leader is not shy in making tough decisions to ensure these values and beliefs are maintained and respected.

This includes standing up for what is right and taking action when you see behavior that is not in line with the values and beliefs of the team (regardless of the source of that action). In summary, the team wants to see that you have their back in this regard.

Conversely, the quickest way to erode, or even destroy trust, is for your own personal actions to be incongruent with your stated values and beliefs. When you act in a way that is, or even perceived to be, misaligned with your stated values and beliefs, trust will disappear quickly. This is something that you may wish to build into your self-reflection practice and keep an eye on.

Asking yourself, "Did I live by my values and beliefs today?" Or "Were my actions in alignment with my values and beliefs?" You could also take the extra step of having an accountability partner for this. Someone in the team that you privately ask you to hold you to account and to let you know if they start seeing any divergence.

Empowerment and Enablement

Two attributes that often go hand-in-hand are the ability to empower (and back) their team and to give them the environment and resources they need to be successful. This can include both providing resources and removing roadblocks and providing a blame-free culture so that people back themselves.

One of my great mentors, Laurent Eskenazi, was exceptional at this. Giving the team the empowerment to get on with these, backing their judgment, and asking what resources they needed.

Without empowerment, teams can quickly become ineffective. Always waiting for approval before acting. This can be severely detrimental to progress, particularly when faced with time critical decisions that need to be made.

Always remember that you are employing people because of the skills and experience they are bringing to the table. It makes no sense to pay a qualified person a good salary and then spend all day telling them what to do and how to do their job.

Accountability and Responsibility balanced with praise

A great leader has the exceptional ability to take full accountability and responsibility of the performance of their team. They will step in front and take the heat when necessary and shoulder any blame for failure (and learn from that failure).

They will then also be the first to praise the team (collectively and individually) for successes as they occur.

A No-Blame Culture - Psychological Safety

A great leader creates a no-blame culture. They create a psychologically safe environment where people can openly voice their opinions, concerns, issues, risks, and failures without fear of judgment or retribution.

Providing a blame-free culture will give people the space they need to back themselves and try out new things.

In turn this creates benefits in a variety of ways including speed of execution (where people do not wait for permission, they just get on with it) and encouraging more innovation in the way they execute.

Some of the keys to a blame free culture include not "shooting the messenger" when you receive bad news and creating a culture that there is "no such thing as failure, only learning experiences" (Tony Robbins).

Chandler Bolt of Self-Publishing School embraces this with his amazing organization with the mantra of "Fail fast, fail forward, fail often." The premise here is that nothing great in this world ever comes from not trying. You try, you fail, you learn, you try again. In fact the only real failure is never trying in the first place.

It is important in a blame-free culture that you are indeed building in that learning cycle and that you are implementing what you learn. This means conducting debriefs at the end of activities or undertakings. This is not too different to our self-reflection exercise described in this book and in The Leadership Project Self-Reflection journal. The difference is that you are doing this as a team.

You are asking similar questions:

1. What went well?
2. What didn't go well?
3. What can we do more of next time?
4. What should we stop doing?
5. What should we do differently?

All conducted with no blame to any individual.

Know when to be the first to speak, when to be the last to speak

One of the greatest attributes of many great leaders is their ability to know when to be the first to speak and when to be the last to speak. Most great leaders default to the latter and try to be the last to speak. Being the last to speak allows your team to have their voice and feel valued and empowered. Furthermore, it allows space for an expansion of ideas as long as possible. As a leader people will always be looking toward you for signals about what you think. If you speak too early people will naturally start gravitating toward your viewpoint with a desire to please you. Also be careful with your body language and facial expressions as they will also be looking for non-verbal signals of which ideas and statements you like and dislike.

This also gives you thinking time. You can continue to listen with an open mind, an open heart, and an open will to everything that is being said and weigh all options up.

A powerful conclusion is to then step in at the crescendo of the meeting with a succinct summary of the most important three things that have been discussed and with guidance on what should be the next steps; in doing so, making sure you appreciated everyone's input and thinking.

You do need to pay close attention throughout and if you see the meeting either deteriorating, spiralling, or stalling you may need to interject from time to time with prompting questions to keep everything moving in a constructive way. You may also need to keep an eye on inclusiveness to make sure that everyone's voice is being heard and give prompts if there are people that you can see have something to say but can't get a word in because of dominant personality or voices in the room. Pay attention to the body language of your team throughout. This will give you a strong indication of where the team gets excited or concerned on different topics or viewpoints. This is the body language of both the speaker and those listening.

While being the last to speak should be the default, there are times where being the first to speak and perhaps the dominant voice in the room is necessary. Examples of this could include during crisis management where people may be looking for strong and decisive leadership at that time. Even in these circumstances still make sure you are getting as many inputs as possible and drive a culture of inclusiveness in the conversation and actions needed.

A leader should also take the lead when declaring the vision, purpose, impact, values and beliefs of the team. Once again, still maintaining that environment of open inclusiveness in the room to ensure that the team is empowered, engaged, and energized. Ensuring that they have a psychologically safe environment to speak their mind and they take a level of team ownership and buy-in of the end result.

Putting It Into Action

Take the time to consider your own leadership attributes.

Take the bold step of sharing them with your team (the strengths and shortcomings). Be very clear, be humble, and be consistent.

Ask your team for their thoughts and provide a safe environment for honest answers. Do they agree with your self-assessment?

Open up and tell your team of your own failures and shortcomings. This shows great humility and strength and builds a strong bond of trust with your team.

Moment of self-reflection

Take a moment now to stop, reflect, and think on the following questions:

1. How would you rate yourself against these leadership attributes?
2. How would you describe your own leadership style?
3. What are your strengths?
4. What are your weaknesses?
5. What are your challenges?
6. What are your failings?
7. What are your values and beliefs?
8. Will you share these with your team?
9. How will you hold yourself accountable to be consistent to these?

Chapter Ten

Be a purpose-driven leader

Finding Your Personal Why

Being a purpose-driven leader relies on understanding and being in touch with your own personal why. Everyone in the world is slightly different, and you will become a better leader if you are able to find your own personal why and drivers. There are generally nine categories of motivation that include topics like "Creating a difference in the world" and "Making sense of the world." There are no right or wrong answers—they are just different. A powerful "why" statement remains rooted in its high-level motivation but becomes increasingly specific as you become more self-aware.

For anyone looking to understand your own personal why, I strongly recommend that you review the work and books of Simon Sinek [12]. Simon has managed to codify this better than anyone else that I have seen. In addition to his books, Simon's team at simonsinek.com also runs workshops, training, and coaching on the power of why, how to discover your why, and how to live your why.

Ikigai and Raison D'être

When exploring your purpose and your personal why, another interesting exercise is to explore the concept of Ikigai.

Ikigai is a Japanese concept similar to the French "Raison D'etre" (reason for being). Ikigai relates to the benefit or worth of being alive. It is said to be the intersection of the following things:

- What you love doing
- What you are good at

- What the world needs (or at least one other human being)
- What you can be rewarded for (most literature on Ikigai has "what you can be 'paid' for." However, I find it important to consider more than just monetary rewards. Yes, you need to earn enough income to put a roof over your head and food on the table, but there are other rewards as well. Intrinsic rewards that bring you great joy and fulfilment.

You may wish to consider what you are doing in your career now against these criteria and whether you are hitting that intersection. Don't rush off to a career change just yet. Consider under what circumstances, and what you would need to adjust, to hit that intersection. If you are in a role that does not hit the markers and you cannot imagine that ever happening, then yes you may wish to start thinking about what other career you could be doing that would achieve this state.

Beyond Ikigai, I highly recommend the works of Zach Mercurio, best-selling author of *The Invisible Leader* [13]. Zach's work will guide you through a process to find your purpose. His process focuses heavily on the impact you have on other human beings. Considering questions like:

- What did I love doing today?
- What was I good at?
- How did I help another human being?

If you are struggling to see how what you do has purpose of meaning, consider what would happen if you simply stopped doing that thing. Consider what would happen if you did more of that thing. If you look closely, purpose and meaning may start emerging right where you are.

Another powerful exercise is to write your purpose statement. Write what you do (a verb), who you do it for (a person/people) and why you do it. The why can be represented as a "so that" statement.

Here is my own personal purpose statement for reference.

I exist to empower leaders with the tools and skills they need so that they can create amazing teams and workspaces. Workspace where people have purpose and meaning in what they do, their voices are heard and opinions and valued, and that everyone feels that they individually and collectively matter.

Finding your values and beliefs

There are multiple ways that you can discover your personal values and beliefs. Consider the things that get you most excited and/or agitated about in the world. What are the statements that get your attention that you can never forget? What are the actions or events that create a deep emotional reaction for you? As you continue to understand these things, your values will become clearer.

Everyone is different, and you should take the time to understand your own personal beliefs and values rather than just copy someone else's. These may also change over time. As you have more life experiences you will begin to notice different emotional reactions to different situations. When you stop, pay attention, and notice and name these things you will discover they are often driven by your personal values.

The "Pleasant Life," the "Good Life," and the "Meaningful Life"

Martin Seligman, the father of Positive Psychology, describes three lives that we pursue [14]:

- The Pleasant Life
- The Good Life
- The Meaningful Life

The Pleasant Life is when we embark on pleasure-seeking activities. Pleasure releases dopamine into our brain and we feel great and happy at that very moment. We get pleasure from things like social media, sex, binge-watching a series on Netflix, etc. The issue with pleasure is that it habituates. It has an increasingly shorter half-life and we become immune over time to its effect. Therefore, to achieve the same level of pleasure from any given activity we have to either increase its amplitude or increase the frequency and duration to get the same effect as the very first time we experienced it. In short, it becomes an addiction that becomes difficult to feed and maintain.

To be clear, I am not saying that you should not seek pleasure and enjoy it, just explaining it so that the difference between pleasure and joy is clear.

The Good Life is when you achieve a flow state. When we are so engrossed in the activity that we are performing that time becomes immaterial. We are completely present, in the moment, and everything else falls away around us. When we are in the midst of an activity or experience and time seems to have become irrelevant, where it no longer feels like work, and where it feels like this is the most important thing you can be doing right now; this is a state of flow. Chess players can often find themselves in this flow state. Consider in your life if you have ever found yourself in a flow state of complete immersion.

The meaningful life is when we are engaged in activities that have true meaning and purpose for us. It is the "meaningful life" that brings true joy and fulfillment.

When we experience joy it has a long lasting effect on us. The feeling of happiness from joy will last well beyond when the activity itself has stopped. It is a feeling of glow and pride. The Meaningful Life can go hand in hand with the experience of a flow state and The Good Life. If you stop and think, you may be able to find some experiences similar to this in your life. We have all heard statements like "Do something that you love and you never have to work a day in your life." Well, this is an extrapolation of what we mean by finding a balance of the "good life" and the "meaningful life."

An interesting thing that comes from the studies of joy and flow state is that for the vast majority of people, joy and flow comes from selfless acts. That joy and happiness that you get when you have helped someone else without seeking anything in return for yourself, from true altruistic philanthropic acts.

My greatest moments of joy come from quietly watching someone that I have been coaching or mentoring bloom and flourish. That may seem strange from an extreme extrovert, but there is nothing more satisfying for me than to watch someone that I have been developing and helping to take the spotlight and shine through. It could be knocking out of the park with a presentation or it could be watching their leadership style come to the surface with their team.

To achieve a balanced life, you may look for elements of all three lives. Life is too short to not have some fun along the way and seek the "pleasant life." Consider this in your teams, what are you bringing to the table to create a fun environment? To achieve lasting joy, we all need to go beyond the "pleasant life" and seek that flow state and to seek that purpose and meaning.

If you do not find joy in your current role, it is not a terminal situation. You may need to take some time to consider the following:

- Take some time to step back and look things from a different perspective
- Break down your role into things that you do enjoy
- Consider where you are bringing value to others
- Consider what you can do more of or less of to maximize your value and impact
- Consider how you can derive joy from where you are before you consider a large career shift

Purpose and Values-Driven Leadership

People want to work for a company or organization that has a clear purpose and creates positive impact. This has always been the case to a certain degree, but it is increasing with each generation. There can be various reasons for that shift, but it appears that purpose and impact now seems to be the number one criteria for millennials and Gen Z when looking to join a new organization.

This could be related to the next generations being less materialistic and more experience driven than previous generations. They also have a strong social consciousness and compass and care deeply about societal issues such as racism, equity, equality, and the environment. This means that they may not have the same level of loyalty to a company if they find the organization they joined was not who they expected they would be. This will make it increasingly difficult to attract and retain new talent into organizations. It will also mean increased churn on your team and increased costs associated with onboarding and team performance. Conversely, if you are crystal clear about your purpose and impact you will attract and retain a talented, dedicated, and loyal team that sees the value they are bringing to the world.

One of the key transitions I made in my career was when I moved to Hong Kong to lead the Asia Pacific business of Thales Revenue Collection Systems. Not long after my arrival, I stood up in front of the entire Thales Hong Kong business (all business lines) and shared my personal story. I was very clear about my personal vision for the world and about my personal values and beliefs.

I shared with the group my vision for creating a world where people can move freely around their cities, without congestion, without delays, and ultimately without stress. That I wanted to remove the stress from everyone's daily commute. Remove the stress of not knowing whether it would take 40 minutes to get to work or more than four hours, the stress and fear that they might miss an important flight, and the stress of not being able to get home in a timely manner at the end of the day to spend more time with their families. I also spent time to openly declare my personal values and beliefs.

Immediately at the end of that speech I had no less than three senior leaders from other parts of the Thales business pulling me aside and asking how they can be part of that vision. As the week progressed, I had more than 30 emails and resumes from members of the Thales organization that wanted to be on board. I did not give this speech as a recruiting drive, but it demonstrated to me first-hand the power of having a clear personal vision, values, and beliefs that you are very open about.

This experience has repeated itself multiple times in my career. When I led the establishment and launch of the Umo Mobility business within Cubic, I had an identical but amplified reaction from people in the business with people from both Cubic Transportation Systems and Cubic Defense Systems businesses contacting me wanting to be part of that journey. The same is also true on the conclusion of presentations at international conferences where I have been very open about my personal vision.

Most recently, this occurred again when I founded The Leadership Project. The vision of The Leadership Project is to Inspire All Leaders to Challenge the Status Quo. I speak openly that I believe that leadership practices have not kept pace with the modern world and that I want to create a world where people love their jobs, feel valued, respected, and wanted and actually like their bosses. A world based on psychological safety and purpose-driven teams. Each and every time I express the vision and purpose of The Leadership Project I get similar reactions about this vision really resonating with people and people asking how they can get involved. In one notable case, a respected Master Coach and Employment Lawyer said that she had goosebumps listening to it.

Why am I sharing this with you? I am sure it does not sound humble (which is quite unusual for me). I am sharing this because it is becoming increasingly universally accepted now that most people want to follow leaders that have a shared vision, values, and beliefs to their own views.

These examples have shown the ability to attract and retain new talented staff members simply by being very clear about your own personal why, about what drives and motivates you, and about your vision of the world you are trying to create. By being very clear about your values and beliefs.

Well beyond this, you end up with a team that is motivated and inspired by the cause. A motivated and inspired team will be able to achieve feats beyond your wildest dreams. They will go above and beyond at almost every turn because they believe in the mission and that they are working on something that is bigger and more important than themselves.

I encourage you to share your values and beliefs with your team early and often. Be very open with them from your earliest exchanges and reinforce them periodically. Also remember to share your values and beliefs with new team members when they join.

One of my all-time favorite quotes from Simon Sinek that summarizes this perfectly is as follows:

"If you hire people just because they can do a job, they'll work for your money. But if you hire people who believe what you believe, they'll work for you with blood and sweat and tears."

Everyone in the world has different motivations. By being very clear about your own, you will find people that have similar values and motivations will naturally gravitate toward you.

Building and Retaining Trust

The key to building and retaining trust is to be unwaveringly consistent in your vision, values, and beliefs. Being consistent builds and retains trust in your team. This means making sure that you are consistent and persistent in your communication of your vision, values, and beliefs within your organization, with your customers, and with your stakeholders. The continuity of message will keep people motivated and focused on the bigger picture. In repeating your message, you must ensure that you maintain that same passion and fire that led you to this vision in the first place and that it does not just become some sort of rehearsed speech. A great test of whether you are being successful with this is to quietly observe and see if other leaders in your business start to repeat the message, but in their own words and with their own stamp on it.

A very rewarding and proud moment in my career has been watching my successor leading the Umo Mobility business, Bonnie Crawford, taking that business from strength to strength. She has fully embraced the original vision, values and beliefs but also added her own personality and her own personal stamp on it. There is almost nothing more rewarding than watching someone champion your original cause but taking it to new heights and achieving even more than you were personally able to achieve.

On the flip side, the fastest way to kill trust in your teams and customers is if your behaviors do not match the vision, values, and beliefs that you have been articulating. Be very careful to test critical decisions against your vision, values, and beliefs and ensure that your actions match.

A practice that I have recently taken up is to document my own personal leadership credo. This is a list of accountability statements describing how I want to show up as a leader. I empower my team with the right to challenge me if they ever see behavior or decisions that are not in line with my credo. They can challenge me without fear of judgment or retribution.

My leadership credo is as follows:

As a leader I:

- Value a diversity of thought
- Create an environment where everyone feels included
- Hold space for, and encourage, growth in my team
- Listen deeply without judgment
- Open Mind, Open Heart (emotion), Open Will
- Am ready to unlearn what I think I already know
- Learn something new every day
- Work on my leadership every day
- Take a genuine interest in the welfare of my team
- Treat people the way they want to be treated
- Maintain awareness of my own emotional state
- Communicate vision and purpose with clarity
- Help each team member to find their purpose and meaning

Putting It Into Action

If you do not already know your personal why and your values and beliefs, then take the time to discover yourself. Look deep into your own personal motivations and look deep and pay attention to things that create the biggest emotional reactions from you.

Openly share these with your team. Do so early and do so often. Being clear about your personal why, your vision, your values, and beliefs will attract people to you that are drawn in by that. To build and maintain trust, you will need to walk the walk and your actions must always be consistent with those values and beliefs.

When considering your personal why, also test it to see if it brings you a flow state and true joy and test it against the concept of Ikigai.

My Personal Why

You will see above that my personal why has changed slightly over the years, but if you look closely, it hasn't really. The "why" has not changed, only the vehicle by which I look to effect that particular why has changed.

My deep rooted why is to "create a meaningful impact in the world by making people's lives less stressful and happier." It is driven by a desire that nobody deserves to feel stressed all the time and that people deserve to be happy and fulfilled.

With my focus on mobility - I look to remove stress from people's daily commute so they can spend more quality time doing what they love.

With my focus on leadership - I look to remove stress in people's work lives. We are spending up to a third of our lives in jobs that we don't love, and this is a human tragedy. I believe with conviction that we can make people's lives far less stressful, more enjoyable, and more fulfilling through exceptional leadership at all levels of an organization.

So, the why hasn't changed, but the means of achieving it has expanded.

My personal why is still about making a positive impact in the world and making people's lives happier and less stressful, but the focus has shifted to the workplace.

My personal why now is to create a world where people truly love their jobs, have rewarding careers based on purpose and impact, and where they work in organizations and teams that make them feel they belong, feel valued, and feel that they matter.

My Personal Values and Beliefs

Tapping into the things that get me most passionate (upset, angry or joyful) I am able to deeply understand my values and beliefs. I then very openly and transparently share these with my team and with anyone ready to listen.

1. **Equity and Equality.** I believe in equity and equality and want to see an end to any form of discrimination. We are all created equally and there is no place for discrimination in this world. This includes the end of any form of harassment, which is often driven by some level of bias (conscious or unconscious).

2. **Diversity of Thought.** I believe in diversity of thought. I believe that all problems and issues in the world are best solved by collecting a diverse set of viewpoints from people of all walks of life and perspectives

3. **Inclusiveness Everywhere.** I believe that everyone wants to belong. They want to belong to something bigger than themselves. Everyone deserves to feel included. No one deserves to feel excluded. Exclusion is wrong on many levels. No one deserves that awful feeling of not belonging or not being welcomed (I am sure you have all felt that at some point in your life). This is not good for the mental health of that individual. Furthermore, it is bad for business and bad for the team if someone does not feel included. An excluded person is not going to be highly motivated by the common cause, they are highly unlikely to bring their best every day, and are highly unlikely to speak up if they have a wonderful idea. Inclusion also means making sure that people's voices are heard. This was beautifully summarized by Kimberley Abbott in her interview on The Leadership Project podcast [15] when she said, "Getting women a seat at the table is not enough; we need to ensure their voices are heard and valued." You could take this beautiful statement and replace that word with "people" or any *group* of people, and it would still ring true.

4. **Openness and Transparency.** I believe in creating a culture based on open and transparent communication. Openness and transparency builds and maintains trust.

5. **Psychologically Safe Environment.** I believe in creating a psychologically safe environment with a blame-free culture. One where people feel safe to express their opinions, thoughts, issues, and problems without fear of criticism, judgment, or retribution.

6. **Empathy and Connection.** I believe in taking the time to truly know someone and treat them the way they want to be treated (the Platinum Rule). Connecting with people means taking a genuine interest in people and ensuring they feel they are valued and that they matter.

7. **Engagement.** I believe in involving and engaging people in any situation will achieve greater ownership and a greater result. This includes having a coaching mindset and teaching people how to think. Taking them on a journey of self-discovery so they find the answer themselves rather than just providing the answer. If they do find that answer through self-discovery, they will remember it forever; if I tell them the answer, they will remember it for the day and will forget as soon as that information is no longer useful to them. Engagement also means inspiring someone to do something because they want to do it, not because they were told to and to involve them so they are part of the solution.

Moment of self-reflection

Take a moment now to consider:

1. Can you think of inspirational leaders that you have followed before?
2. Were they clear about their vision, values, and beliefs?
3. Do you know your personal why?
4. Do you clearly articulate your personal vision, values, and beliefs?
5. Can you express these with persistent, consistent, and passionate communication?
6. Are your actions and decisions consistent with this vision, these values, and these beliefs at all times?
7. Do you have a way of being held accountable to them?
8. Do you have joy in your life and a state of flow? Or are you in a constant pleasure-seeking cycle?
9. Do you find that what you do today aligns with your personal why, brings you joy, and hits the intersection of your Ikigai?

Chapter Eleven

Empathy and Leadership

Empathy and Leadership

It is often said that if you are struggling to see someone else's point of view, you should walk a mile in their shoes. That way, if you still do not agree with them, you are a mile away, and you have their shoes. Kidding, of course.

Every single person on this planet is different in some way, and that is a beautiful thing. We are different in our backgrounds, experiences, and genetic make-up. We are also very different in terms of personal motivators, stressors, and preferences.

To illustrate the point, picture a Town Hall meeting of your company where two people (let's call them Susan and Franck) are up for a well-deserved recognition for all of the work they have been doing to move the company forward in its vision.

They are both brought up on the stage, presented an award by the chairman and CEO to a room full of their proud (and maybe jealous) colleagues that are clapping, hooting, and cheering loudly. Before too long, the murmuring and then chanting of "Speech, speech, speech," starts to spread around the crowded room.

Sounds like an amazing moment for most people. But pause for a moment.

What if I told you that Susan is an extreme extrovert and loves nothing more than the spotlight, attention, and adoration of her teammates.

What if I told you Franck is a deeply introverted person who, while still deeply proud of his achievements, would rather be anywhere else than here at this very moment. This is his worst nightmare, public speaking is his greatest fear, and he is starting to physically shake.

For Susan, it is mission accomplished. She deserves to be rewarded and could not be happier. A smile is beaming from cheek to cheek, she is cherishing every moment, and wants it to go on forever.

For Franck, we have a deep, deep problem. A moment of pride has turned into thoughts of "What did I do to deserve this?" "How do I get out of here?" and "How do I prevent this from ever happening again?"

Breaking the Golden Rule

For many years, in leadership training and in everyday life, people have been taught The Golden Rule.

"Treat others the way you want to be treated."

I trust that our story above about Susan and Franck is illustration enough that this approach is very limiting. There are circumstances where this might apply. For example, it could be the "default" for when you do not know someone too well.

However, I strongly encourage you to move past The Golden Rule as quickly as possible and get yourself to The Platinum Rule.

The Platinum Rule

The Platinum Rule trumps The Golden Rule every time.

"Treat others the way *they* want to be treated."

This means that you need to truly take the time to get to know your team.

1. What are their likes and dislikes?
2. What are their working-style preferences?
3. How do they like to be managed?
4. How do they like to receive feedback and constructive criticism?
5. How do they like to be rewarded?
6. What motivates them?
7. What stresses them out?

This is perhaps the most important thing a team leader can do to lift their ability to inspire their team. People truly appreciate when someone takes a genuine interest in them and how they like to work.

To circle back to our story. Franck may have preferred a nice dinner, a book, or even a day off rather than to stand on that stage.

This goes deeper than just rewards and recognition and should influence your daily interactions with your team.

Don't Make Assumptions

It is critically important that you don't make assumptions on their behalf and that you actually check in with the person. Ask them about their preferences and give them a psychologically safe environment to provide an open and transparent answer. This means listening without judgment, paying close attention to what they are saying, and using active listening and summarizing to show to them that you heard and understood them.

This will go a very long way to building a strong connection with them and showing them that they matter.

Personality Traits and Profiling

The world of psychology is full of different forms of profiling tools and techniques each measuring people across different scales including personality traits, personal preferences, and levels of emotional intelligence.

Some of the more common ones include Myers Briggs Type Indicator (MBTI), DISC profiling, Enneagram, Lifestyles Inventory, Clifton Strength Finder, EQi 2.0, and Hogan Profiling, but there are many more than this. There are many sources of additional information on personality preferences and profiling.

At The Leadership Project, we could help you with an EQi assessment as one of our favored tools for helping our clients improve their emotional intelligence and self-awareness.

For MBTI, I would highly recommend reaching out to Gary Williams of Better Future International (as featured in The Leadership Project podcast episode 32 [16]) as he specializes in this field.

MBTI is perhaps the most common and measures people's preferences across four scales to produce 16 different type indicators as follows:

- (E)xtroversion vs (I)ntroversion
- (S)ensing vs I(N)tuition
- (T)hinking vs (F)eeling
- (J)udging vs (P)erceiving

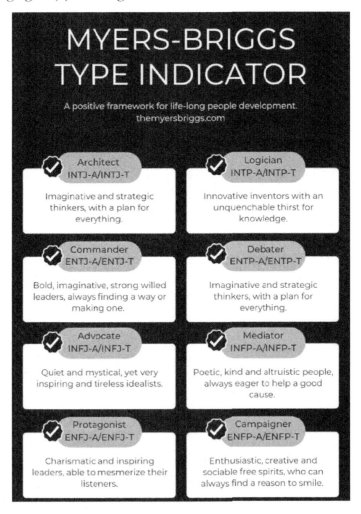

These profiling tools and techniques can provide valuable information about your own personal preferences and the preferences of your team. You may wish to do an exercise as a team using one of the personality profiling techniques to get to know each other more deeply and build empathy among the team.

This is an exercise that I did, with the great help of Ross Nicol, at the early stages of the Auckland project. During our kick-off meeting and team-building workshop, we conducted an open group exercise exploring each other's personality preferences. This led to a much deeper understanding of each other. Subsequently setting the groundwork for how we would communicate with each other and inspire the team into great and meaningful action.

It can also help the leader to understand whether they have balance in the team to drive diversity of thought. Not to overthink this, but still an interesting indicator for the leader to consider.

However, be careful to note that these are **preferences** and do not necessarily represent **skills** that the person may have. So, be careful not to over-emphasize or make decisions based on profile and preferences alone.

A great example of a mismatch between skills and preferences is Simon Sinek. Simon is an inspirational and impactful speaker and orator when presenting to a large group of people. So, you may be surprised to hear that Simon is in fact an Introvert. So, his natural preference for introversion is not an indication of his incredible ability to capture the attention of an audience with expertly delivered speeches and presentations.

Another example would be myself. I am an ENTJ. This would mean that I have a normal preference for wanting some level of order and structure in the world and to be able to explain the world rationally. However, after studying people, psychology, and emotional intelligence I have learned to understand that the world (and people) are often not rational. With my focus on emotional self-awareness and understanding the emotions of others, you may consider on the surface that I am an ENFP. However, my study on topics like emotional intelligence has been to help me make rational sense of an irrational world and emotional self-awareness and understanding the impact of emotions is something that I have learned over time. I could also note that I am at the extreme end of extroversion and gain great energy from my interactions with other people, but one could argue that if I was not able to put those preferences aside I would never be able to dedicate the alone time needed to write this very book.

The lesson here is to not take personality and preference profiling on face value. Discuss it with the team member and make your own observations around skills and value.

It is also important to note that each of these MBTI categories are a scale and most people will be somewhere on that scale rather than be at the extreme end of each category.

While MBTI and other instruments can provide valuable information about personal preferences you do need to be careful with regard to how they are used. Begin with making sure you always have a clear reason for using the tool before embarking on it. Consider how you are going to use the outcomes before you begin any testing.

I see many organizations use tools like MBTI during the recruitment process. If this is just simply as one piece of information then this is okay, but I would not recommend using it as a basis for a recruitment selection for the skills vs preferences examples listed above. Simon Sinek would never get a gig as a speaker, and if that were the case and the world would be missing out.

Be careful not to use type indicators and preference profiles as a way to "explain" someone's behavior. A typical example of this is where team members might start statements with qualifiers like "Because I am an INFP, I decided to…" or projecting that on to others: "You only said that because you are a Type 4 on your Enneagram."

Also be careful with language that may be used around this. A memorable moment in my career was when one financial controller took deep offense to someone saying, "Oh, that's because you are a control freak," with humorous intent after a profiling exercise but not taken well. The quick response was "Yes, I may have a preference for control, but that doesn't make me a freak."

In summary, profiling tools and techniques can provide valuable information and help build understanding and empathy. However, always make sure you are using them for the right reasons and take care to make sure the results are not inappropriately handled.

Customer Empathy Map

Another powerful tool for understanding the motivations, emotions, and preferences of people is the Customer Empathy Map. As the name implies this is typically used with customers in mind. However, there is no reason why this cannot be used with any stakeholder (your team, your boss, or other teams).

The process asks you to put yourself in place of that person and consider the following:

- Their goals
- What they think
- What they feel
- Their pains
- What gains they seek
- What do they DO, HEAR, SEE, and SAY

Whether you use this tool formally or just learn from it, there is something interesting here for you and your leadership approach.

For formatter - insert Customer Empathy Map and reference to it.

Take the time now and consider how you could implement The Customer Empathy Map as part of your leadership toolkit. Take each member of your team and consider the world from their perspective. Write their name at the top, imagine the world from their role and with their preferences in mind. What do they do, hear, see and say? Most importantly, what do they think and feel? What are their pains and challenges? What does success look like for them?

The Power of Perspective

Perspective is EVERYTHING.

As you develop these skills in empathy and understanding, your will also unlock the power of perspective.

Perspective may be the most powerful skill that you can develop as a leader. I am certain you have heard the saying "There are always two sides to every story." Well, that doesn't go far enough. In any situation there are always multiple angles, perspectives, and lenses through which you can see the world. These translate into perceptions that people will develop as their own "truth" of the situation. Many times, that "truth" they hold will seem illogical to you. That is, until you step back and look at the situation from different angles.

I encourage you to try this exercise from time to time. When there is a perplexing situation, try removing yourself from the picture. Take a "fly on the wall" or "helicopter" view of the situation and see what you notice. Then, look at the situation from each stakeholder's viewpoint. How do they see the situation? How do they see themselves in that situation? How do they see you and others? People's perceptions of themselves, their perceptions of the world around them, and their perceptions of others, play an important factor in how they make decisions, how they act, and how they feel.

Doing this exercise of looking through different lenses and perspectives will often result in aha moments of understanding for you.

Once you begin to master this skill of perspective it can also become an incredibly powerful tool to use with your team. Imagine you have a situation where you believe one of your team members is being close minded. You can walk them through a perspective exercise to open their mind to new ideas and new truths. Is it also a powerful tool when managing conflict between two team members. Getting them to stop and look at each other's perspective, but also get them to perceive how their conflict may be affecting others around them.

Moment of self-reflection

Take a moment now to stop, reflect, and think with the following questions:

1. Do you take the time to truly get to know your team?
2. Do you understand their preferences?
3. Do you understand what makes them tick and motivates them?
4. Do you understand how they like to be treated?
5. What level of direction and delegation do they prefer?
6. How do they prefer to be rewarded?
7. Do you take the time each day to ask people how they are?
8. Do you take a genuine interest in the answer?
9. Do you test assumptions before concluding what you think someone else's "agenda" and motivations are?
10. Have you considered using any profiling techniques on your team?
11. If so, how will you use the results?
12. Have you considered looking at the world and the situation through different lenses and perspectives?
13. What emerged from these multiple perspectives?
14. How will you use this emerging knowledge?
15. How will you use perspective as a skill in your toolkit?

Chapter Twelve

Emotional Intelligence

The Emotionally Intelligent Leader

"People don't care how much you know, until they know how much you care." - Teddy Roosevelt.

Leadership is all about how we relate to other people. Emotional Intelligence (or EQ) is at the heart of how we relate to other people.

Emotional Intelligence relates to our ability to perceive, control, use, and evaluate emotions. This includes our emotions and the emotions of others.

Emotional Intelligence (or EQ) is a field of study that we continue to learn more and more about, and I encourage you to make a focus on EQ a part of your developmental path. Daniel Goleman, the author of multiple books on Emotional Intelligence [17] has demonstrated through his studies that it is EQ, not IQ, that is a more accurate indicator of someone's future success. Studies (formal and informal) consistently show that people that rise to the top of the ranks in all fields are not necessarily those with academic prowess. The valedictorian of your school or university is not typically the one that rises to the top of their chosen field after school. There is a long list of incredibly successful people that never even graduated from their chosen field of studies. The same is also true with regard to leadership skills, as many of the most inspirational and respected leaders that you will encounter don't necessarily have the highest IQ in the room.

So, what do all of these leaders have in common if it is not a high IQ? It is their ability to relate to others. Their ability to empathize and understand all of the people they are interacting with including team members, customers, peers, their own bosses, everyone. This is what truly sets them apart.

So, why is that so? One of my favorite quotes is an African Proverb:

"If you want to go fast, go alone; if you want to go far, go together."

This sums up the importance of emotional intelligence perfectly. IQ can be a great driver of your individual performance and how good you are at your chosen field or domain of work. However, EQ provides you with the skills to be able to interact with a larger group of people and to inspire them to achieve amazing things. This, in turn, has a multiplication effect. Rather than just the efforts of one person, we now have the efforts of a collection of people all motivated by the same vision and direction. All supporting each other to reach far greater heights than any individual could achieve.

I have some really good news for you. Unlike IQ, EQ is something that you can improve on over time. IQ is something that is more or less stable throughout your entire life, whereas EQ is something that you can actively work on. If you have not previously done so, I encourage you all to consider undertaking an EQ-i assessment. There are many certified suppliers of EQ-i assessments that you can choose from, including my team at The Leadership Project. EQ-i helps you to measure your current state across a range of categories. A trained EQ-i assessor will then be able to help you interpret the results and develop an action plan to help you build upon and leverage your strengths and work on any areas where improvement would be beneficial.

For my own personal story and journey, I must admit that this took me a while to work out. Without meaning to boast, I am blessed with a high IQ, and for many years I did believe that this was what was driving my personal success. I would often find myself being able to very quickly solve problems and have greater critical reasoning skills in comparison to others around me. I often thought that people came to me for guidance and direction for this reason. For my domain knowledge, my expertise and for my problem solving abilities. Then, in more recent times, I discovered that it was my ability to interact with others, to understand them, to meet them where they are. It was my ability to bring them along their own journey of discovery and self-development that was driving my success. I was not being successful because of my own personal abilities, I was being successful because I have the ability to understand others and to inspire them to do what they do. To inspire and support them to become the best versions of themselves. As per the African proverb, I was being successful because of the collective power of the people that I was surrounding myself with. My domain skill and knowledge was just an added bonus and not the determining factor in that success.

The other life-changing moment for me was when I discovered and studied the psychology of decision making. This started with Simon Sinek and his groundbreaking work and his book "Start with Why" and understanding how great leaders and brands inspire people into action [12]. At the root of this is neuroscience and understanding that people make decisions emotionally and then justify them rationally, not the other way around. The further I looked into this the more I understood it was true. This leads to understanding buying behavior and the process that someone goes through when they decide to make a purchase and then when they decide who they are going to make that purchase with. People buy from people (or brands) that they know, like, and trust and all of these factors relate to the emotions or feelings they have toward that person or brand. They may then justify that purchase rationally with statements like "this car has the best safety features in the market," but in reality they made an emotional decision to begin with and now they are justifying it.

The same then goes with leadership. People will follow leaders that they know, like and trust. They will follow leaders because of their vision and purpose, values, and beliefs, and not because of their academic credentials. They will follow leaders based on their emotions and how that leader makes them feel. How that leader makes them feel about themselves and how they feel about the vision and mission.

To take this to the next level, the performance of those individuals dramatically improves when they are being inspired to do something because they want to do it, not because they were told to do it. William Glasser explained with clarity in his groundbreaking book *Choice Theory* [5] that people have five needs. The needs for:

- Survival

- Love & belonging
- Power
- Fun
- Freedom

This element of Freedom is key here. It is the freedom to make their own choices. It is freedom from oppression. People need to feel that they are in control of their own lives and decisions. To feel they have control of the steering wheel of their life. *Choice Theory* unlocks the power of knowing that people want to feel that they made a conscious choice in their actions and not just doing something because someone (e.g. their boss, their parents) told them to do it.

At the root of all this is emotion and therefore an emotional intelligent and aware leader is always going to be more successful than just an academically intelligent leader.

Self-Awareness, Self-Management, Self-Motivation

"Anyone can become angry—that is easy, but to be angry with the right person, to the right degree, at the right time, for the right reasons, and in the right way—this is not easy." - Aristotle.

This quote from Aristotle perhaps sums up emotional intelligence better than any other quote I have found. Emotional Intelligence is not about ignoring emotion or not showing emotion in any way. It is about using the right emotion at the right time and in the right way.

The ability to understand one's own emotional triggers and emotions is one of the most valuable discoveries any leader can make.

An emotionally intelligent leader is able to notice and name their emotions. They will ask questions like:

- What is this emotion?
- Why am I feeling this emotion?
- Why am I feeling this emotion now?

Just this initial step of asking these questions to yourself enables your ability to regulate your emotions and ensure they are not unduly impacting your decision making.

"Never make a permanent decision based on a temporary emotion." - TD Jakes

Beyond that comes the ability to control one's emotions. This does not necessarily mean to ignore or bury those emotions, but rather to acknowledge and name them and use them in the most appropriate manner the current situation requires.

A great leader is able to determine which emotions are serving them well and which are not serving them well and to control your own reactions to those emotions. There is a time and a place for a controlled release of emotion to show vulnerability or to make it clear to your team what is important to you. There is also a time to keep that emotion contained (for that moment) and to observe as the situation unfolds and don't be too quick to show your hand. Remember that people are always looking for the leader's reaction (verbal and non-verbal) and if you show your emotion too early you may inadvertently influence everything that happens from that moment onward.

The best way to summarize all of this is think about how you "respond" rather than "react" to any emotion or situation in front of you. An immediate "reaction" may not serve you well, but a measured and controlled response most likely will.

This takes time and practice to get right, and you may wish to take on the services of a coach to guide you through this. Take the time to check the credentials of the coach you select. They should be certified by a recognized body such as the International Coaching Federation (ICF). ICF has stringent training and practice requirements that ensure the quality and efficacy of the support you will be receiving. There are many coaches out there that have received no training at all or have been on a three-day course with no assessment criteria and then market themselves as a coach but have little substance. For the avoidance of doubt, it takes much more than three days or a conference to learn and practice the skills of coaching.

I would also encourage all leaders to have their own emotional outlets that you can rely on. Keeping yourself in check, without reaction and without judgment in meetings for long periods of time can be emotionally draining and physically exhausting. Always remember that you are a human being too. Having a great confidant (or even your coach) where you can have emotional outlets can be very good for your mental wellbeing and long-term health. This is not a place to complain about your team or a place of judgment, just an outlet. If you don't already have a confidant, consider who you may call upon for this. Have an open discussion with them. Tell them upfront, "Hey, I just need to vent for a bit, can you listen without judgment. Don't need you to solve anything or help; I just need to vent." It is important to say this upfront because if you pick a friend that deeply cares about you, their natural tendency will be to want to help you, and then you would have transferred some of that emotion and stress to them without reason.

The summary here is to understand your own emotional triggers and your own emotions and then have responses (not reactions) to use this for appropriate effect.

Beyond self-awareness and self-management, highly effective people are able to harness emotion to its full effect through self-motivation. The process of self-motivation is to make that emotion you are feeling work *for* you instead of against you. A great example of this is stress. Many of you will recognise that you work better in stressful situations. Stress can arouse you into motivated action. The key here is to find the optimal stress level for you. We are all different here, and you need to closely observe what works best. Without some stress, you might find yourself cruising in your comfort zone with no real action. Too much stress and you may freeze. Too much stress over a sustained period of time may make you ill. The key is balance and making stress work for you.

Another concept for you to consider is that the emotions you feel are to trying to tell something about a need. A positive emotion is indicating that a need has been met and you are being rewarded for that need to encourage you to do that thing again sometime. This could the need for love & belonging; the need for fun, etc. A negative emotion is indicating a need that has not been met. This could be the need for survival, for love & belonging, for freedom from oppression, etc. When you experience strong emotion takes some time to consider what need has been meet or unmet.

Perceiving the emotion of others - Empathy

Beyond Self-Awareness, Self-Management, and Self-Motivation, Emotional Intelligence also relates to your ability to be able to perceive the emotions of others.

There are primarily three different types of empathy:

- **Cognitive Empathy** - the ability to understand someone else's point of view. This does not necessarily mean that you agree with that person, but that you can see the world through their eyes. You can see and recognize what they are perceiving.
- **Emotional Empathy** - the ability to understand what someone else is feeling.
- **Empathic Concern** - the desire to want to do something to help that person with what they are feeling or the issues they are dealing with.

This empathy can come in multiple forms but must start with the act of paying attention. This means paying attention to body language, choice of words, and other reactions to the situation.

Be on the alert for all kinds of reactions and responses to different stimuli from all of the people that you interact with including customers, stakeholders, team members, peers, and your own boss or bosses. You are looking for their emotional reaction—how they are saying things, how they are reacting, rather than just what they are saying. The emotion is far more important than the content itself.

The leader needs to develop this skill to be able to perceive what is resonating in others and what is not. Be on the lookout for puzzled looks on their faces, pleasure, displeasure, disdain, delight, etc, etc. You then need to ensure that you are connecting and deeply understanding that other person.

This can be further benefited from testing assumptions and asking questions. This can involve being quite direct at times: "Jason, you seemed to have a reaction there, can I ask what happened just there for you?" The skill is to ask questions that show no judgment and to listen to the answer without judgment.

For all of this to be successful, you need to be in the moment and practicing mindfulness and deep listening. Pay attention to all cues (verbal and non-verbal). Deeply listen without judgment, and keep an open mind, open heart, and open will to what you are seeing and hearing.

There will be many times when you are thinking that another person is reacting in an emotional state and not being rational. Some key things that I always remind myself when faced with this situation include:

1. Their perception of the situation is very real for them. It is their reality even if it doesn't seem rooted in fact.
2. If their reaction or position seems to be irrational, it is because it is *not* rational—it is emotional.
3. What part of their brain do I currently perceive they are engaging? This is a much deeper topic for another day, but to keep it simple for now. The frontal cortex is responsible for rational thought, the limbic brain is responsible for emotion (and decision making) and the reptilian brain is responsible for survival instinct (e.g. Fight or Flight). If someone is engaging their reptilian brain because they feel threatened there is a high risk of an extreme response, and you want to defuse that as soon as possible or pause until calm has returned. One technique is to just state, "Okay, it seems like this situation has upset you greatly. I propose that we take a break and a few deep breaths and come back to this in an hour from now." It is critical to put a timeframe on this. You do not want it to drag on and fester, and you do not want the other person to feel that the situation is unresolved and with no plan for how resolution will be found.

The sooner one makes the realization that human beings are emotionally driven and not rational, the sooner you will indeed be able to make sense of the world around you.

A deeper look at EQ-i

I strongly encourage all leaders and aspiring leaders to consider undergoing an EQ-i assessment with an EQ-i trained coach who can help you to interpret the results and put an action plan together. You may wish to have all of your team members to do the same. The one word of advice I have here is that the relationship between that team member and the coach should be a personal and private relationship. I would advise not to insist on seeing the results. Many of your team will gladly share their results and action plan with you, particularly if you have provided a psychologically safe environment for them to do so. It is a far better situation for them to volunteer to share their results with you and take ownership of them, than for you to "insist" on seeing them.

With these results, willingly shared with you, you will be able to have a meaningful conversation with your team member. Ask them what they are seeing in the results? Are they surprised by anything? This will help you to test their self-awareness and willingness to grow. You can have a productive conversation about what strengths they perceive and how they may convert these strengths into superpowers. You can discuss any areas where they did not score as well and hear from them what they can and will do with this increased self-awareness. Please note that having a weakness does not always mean that you need to improve in that area. Sometimes the power comes from just being aware of that weakness and adjusting around it. For example, relying on others to help you with those areas.

It is important to note the interrelationships between different EQ-i categories. An abundance of strength in one area can be detrimental to others. What we are looking for here is balance.

From a leadership perspective, EQ-i examines four different dimensions that align with some of the attributes that people look for in highly successful leaders as follows:

1. Authenticity
2. Coaching
3. Insight
4. Innovation

The EQ-i model looks at behaviors and preferences across five different categories that can drive success:

Self-Perception

Self-perception begins with considering your own self-regard. How do you see and respect yourself and how accepting you are of your own strengths and weaknesses. Do you respect yourself? If you do not respect yourself, it is very hard for others to do so. Are you ready to accept that you do have strengths and weaknesses? (You are human.)

Self-actualization then relates to how you engage yourself in pursuit of your own personal desires toward a fulfilling and meaningful life.

Self-awareness is the ability to truly understand one's own emotions and your own emotional triggers. This is not easy for everyone and can take some time to build. The first step is mindfulness and paying attention to oneself.

Self-Expression

Self-expression deals with our ability to process emotions and express ourselves in appropriate ways. Emotional expression is being able to openly express our feelings (keeping an eye on both verbal and non-verbal expression). I am sure you have encountered many occasions where someone's emotion is written all over their face or in their body language irrespective of what is coming out of their mouth.

Assertiveness relates to our ability to speak and communicate with confidence about our feelings and beliefs in an appropriate manner.

Independence relates to our ability to be self-directed and not just be influenced by the emotions of the group or the people we are with.

Interpersonal

Interpersonal emotional intelligence is at the heart of our ability to recognize, understand and empathize with another person's emotions. This becomes a big determinant factor in your ability to build and maintain trust and to have rewarding relationships with people.

Everyone wants to feel like they matter and they are valued. This goes beyond just listening to what they have to say. It goes to really empathizing and understanding how they feel.

Decision Making

The Decision-Making category relates to your ability to develop sound solutions and problem-solve taking into account the emotions related to the situation.

It includes understanding the emotion but remaining objective throughout the decision-making process. The ability to recognize when emotions or biases may be influencing your own decision making and to take appropriate action.

This category also relates to impulse control and being able to remain patient and take all factors into account before jumping to a conclusion.

This is very challenging. You need to be able to understand emotion and to factor emotion into a decision without losing objectivity.

Stress Management

Stress, at the heart of it, is also an emotion. If you are able to master your own emotional intelligence you will be on your way to having good approaches for managing your own stress levels. Having the flexibility to be able to deal with your own emotions and the emotions of others. Having stress tolerance and turning stress into an optimistic outlook.

Stress is not necessarily a bad thing if it can be appropriately harnessed to optimal performance. Using some level of controlled stress as a way to keep you focused and on point, but having the right mechanisms in place to manage your stress levels for your own mental health.

Balance

An interesting aspect of emotional intelligence is the need for balance across the attributes. It is not necessarily a case that you want to score "off the charts" on every single attribute or measure.

For example, you may need to take great care with balancing emotional self-awareness and self-expression with your stress tolerance, balancing independence with self-awareness, Balancing empathy with self-awareness, and balancing impulse control with stress tolerance.

Your EQ-i coach should be able to provide some good guidance here on how these attributes interrelate with each other.

Putting It Into Action

The best way forward here is to consider an EQ-i assessment for you (or for you and your team) with an EQ-i certified coach. This will be a far more powerful exercise with a certified coach. However, if you do not have the means to engage a coach you can practice some self-assessment against the categories above.

Start considering your own self-awareness of your emotions, your ability to appropriately express those emotions, the ability to read and work with the emotions of others, the ability to appropriately use emotion in decision making while remaining objective and to manage your own stress levels.

If your team has entrusted you with their EQ-i results, you should go to the steps of talking it through with them. You may find that co-sharing your results with them will take your connection, communication, and understanding of each to a whole new level.

Moment of self-reflection

Take a moment now to stop, reflect, and think on your own emotional intelligence:

1. Do you believe you are self-aware of your emotions and emotional triggers?
2. Do you consider the way you express emotion and how that may influence your effectiveness as a leader?
3. Do you take the time to truly understand and empathize with the emotion of others?
4. What steps can you be taking to consider your emotional intelligence and the role it plays in your future as a leader?
5. What actions will you take from this?
6. Have you considered the benefit of undertaking an EQi assessment or coaching in emotional intelligence?

Chapter Thirteen

Communication Skills for Leaders

There are few things more important to a leader than the ability to communicate effectively. There are some pundits that go as far to say that "Communication is leadership" and "Leadership is communication" and it is hard to debate its level of importance.

One of my favourite stories about communication revolves around a married couple. They have been married for 30 years and one of their pleasures in life is to bake their own homemade bread. I am starting to get hungry now as I think about the smell of their kitchen and the waft of freshly baked bread in the air.

Every morning, the husband would pull the bread out from the oven and proceed to slice off the chunky end piece of the bread, put it on a plate, and pass it to his wife.

This goes on every morning for 30 years, until the wife just loses it one day and screams "That's it! I have had enough! I want a divorce!" She takes one deep breath and continues "Every morning for 30 years, you have given me the crusty hard-end piece of the bread. You don't love me. I just can't take it anymore."

With a look of complete bewilderment the husband stammers a reply in shock, "But, that is the best part."

The main moral to this story is about the danger of assumptions (on both sides), but I think it also goes much deeper. It includes thoughts on empathy, and on open and transparent communication, and having confronting conversations.

We have all had leaders that have inspired you through their communication skills and others that have left you confused, bewildered, and unmotivated.

Some key rules to always remember for communication to be effective:

1.   When speaking (or writing) - it is less about what you are saying and more about what the recipient is hearing, understanding, and taking away

2.   When listening - it is less about what you are hearing, and more about what you are understanding.

There are countless times in history (and I am sure in your experience) where two people walk away from a conversation thinking they have a common understanding and consensus only to find out later that they had completely different interpretations of what just happened. The Treaty of Waitangi is a clear example of this. There are countless examples of contractual disputes that highlight the issue. At the team level, it can happen every single day if left unchecked.

So, one of the most important steps in any communication is to summarize and validate understandings. Two of my Amalgam Leaders, Tom Walker and Chris Jenkins, were masters at this. In their ability to be the last to speak and summarize back the most important three things from the meeting. Part of this skill is to isolate the most critical areas where any deviation in common understanding could have more serious consequences. People greatly appreciate this clarity. Beyond just ensuring everyone is on the same page, it also heads off possible conflicts in the team. It also greatly helps to limit nugatory work where people would put in hours of work in a single direction only to find out later that there was a misunderstanding of purpose or direction. You can take this skill to the next level by metaphorically "handing the pen" to one of the team members to act as summarizer. This builds buy-in and extreme ownership of the result. If you are particularly astute you may even pick that one team member who you think may become a future point of resistance to that work. Their entire demeanor changes when they feel they have some say in the course of action.

Communication is a very broad topic, but it does involve everything from:

- Verbal communication
- Formal written communication
- Informal written communication

- Presentations
- Facial expressions
- Even body language

Communication can be as much about what is not said as what is said.

The Danger of Assumptions

To delve straight into the example highlighted in our story, the danger of assumptions is when they go untested. It is human nature to make assumptions, but dangerous to believe they are true without any checking. This can be anything from assuming that someone will like the same things you would like to assuming the intentions of another person. In our story above, I am sure the wife is wondering why her husband, who supposedly loves her, could be so callous as to give her the crusty part of the bread. She was second-guessing his motivations as being selfish (or worse). For his part, the husband assumed that his bride would like the delicious end piece, his favorite part that he had been forgoing for 30 years out of love.

Now, consider this in the business context: what assumptions do you make every day? What assumptions do you make about your team, your customers, the motivations of management? If they go untested, I can guarantee you that at least some things that you believe to be true will indeed not be. Examples of this could include assumed knowledge and thinking that everyone has some level of base knowledge that may not be there. The most dangerous one is assuming someone else's intent without testing that. If you find yourself thinking or verbalizing sentences like, "Bill only said that because he wants to…" or "I think Sally is trying to achieve…" These are clear signals that you are second guessing someone else's motives or goals.

This can also play its way in a negotiation setting. If you do not test your assumptions and motivations about the party you are negotiating with, then you are doing nothing more than guessing what will actually please them and close a win-win deal. In negotiation, if you do not test assumptions about what success looks like from them, you may end up conceding a number of points that were really not that important to them while you search for their "must haves." You can head this off by asking directly what is most critical and immovable for them and by openly sharing your "must haves" with them. All negotiations would be faster and more fruitful for all parties if everyone just openly states their needs rather than trying to second guess each other.

The Law of Attraction

There was much fanfare about the Law of Attraction a few years back with people divided into two camps: avid believers and cynics. I will not delve into the whole concept, but will highlight one key part that relates to communications and assumptions. One of the key elements of the Law of Attraction is about how you prepare your mental state for a meeting. In my experience, if you go into any meeting with untested assumptions about the motivations and intentions of the meeting you are going into, it is almost invariably going to impact the outcome. You need to find ways to test those assumptions either before the meeting or at the start of the meeting so this does not adversely impact the rest of the conversation.

It is like a little twist on Henry Ford's famous saying:

"Whether you think you can, or think you can't, you are probably right."

In the meeting context, if you go into a meeting thinking the worst, then the meeting is most likely going to go poorly. If you go into a meeting thinking it will go well, more often than not it probably will.

One thing you do have to be careful with here is also confirmation bias and only hearing what you want (or think) you heard. Many a meeting in history has resulted in both parties walking away from the meeting with a different interpretation of what had just happened. Same meeting, different perspective. Examples of this could include going into a sales call where you are certain there will be a positive outcome, and you only hear those things that support your case for a sale, and you fail to hear the customer telling you what would be needed to close the deal. Another example would be going into a meeting thinking that another person doesn't like you and you only hearing things that support your view and not hearing the praise they share.

The best way to combat confirmation bias is to practice active listening, deep listening, and summarizing back what you have heard. Be present and in the moment and ensure that you are seeing the whole of the person. Keep an open mind, open heart, and open will about where the conversation may take you. Summarize back and the person will most likely correct you if you miss something important to them in your summary.

So testing assumptions is important at the start of a meeting, testing common understanding is critical at its conclusion.

Multi-sensory communication

As referenced above, communication is absolutely a multi-sensory activity. When communicating we need to pay attention to everything in front and around us. I am not saying that you need to become an expert at body language or facial expressions, but these are key factors.

Human beings find it very difficult to truly hide their emotions, thoughts, and beliefs if you are paying enough attention. To connect with someone on a deep level, to understand them and to build their trust, being in touch with multi-sensory communication is something I strongly encourage you to build.

Pay attention to facial expressions. You may wish to do some training on this, and there are some games and apps that help you to build this skill. An example is PEAK that has a number of different games to help with your cognitive development including one that asks you to be able quickly determine if someone is indeed smiling. It can be challenging to be able to pick up micro-expressions, but they can provide great signals as to whether the person you are communicating with is excited, happy, confused, agitated, worried, etc. If you pick up a sign of confusion, you can then explore that confusion and clarify it straight away.

Body language is a little easier but is also a science in its own right. Body language provides a great signal as to whether someone is fully engaged, mindful, and in the moment of your conversation. By paying attention you will be able to see if they are distracted, would rather be somewhere else, or are just plain uncertain and questioning the current course of action.

The power of language and intonation

Speech patterns become valuable pieces of information. People will often be completely oblivious to this, but you can quickly pick up what is most important to them through the language they use. Intonation and volume of speech, even speed of speech can give signals of emotion and importance. A very rapid and snappy response to a question will typically indicate some level of frustration or a point of agitation. A very long pause, potentially with eyes diverted away, would indicate the other person is going into a reflective state and they may be about to share something deep and meaningful to them. If you see this occurring, be silent and still and let them flow. You may be on the verge of uncovering something very important and potentially connected to their values.

Repeated words or phrases also indicate high levels of significance.

One of the keys to look out for are adjectives and adverbs. Adjectives are descriptive words typically attached to a noun (for example, "this is of huge importance to me," where huge is the adjective). Adverbs are descriptive words attached to verbs (for example, "runs slowly," where slowly is the adverb).

By paying attention to clarifying words and joining words, you will soon learn how important something is to somebody and whether there is some flexibility there or not. This can be a great sign as to whether a point is a "nice to have" or a "must have" for them. Some clear examples are the difference between "must" and "should." If you are not paying attention you will miss this. If someone is saying "should" they are subtly giving away that is not it is not super critical for them.

As you go deeper into this, you start discovering other unusual things. For a reason unknown to myself, when someone is starting a new conversation, and in those first opening stanzas, they will often give away what is most important to them or what is troubling them, but it won't be the first thing they say. My supposition here is that in the start of that conversation they are subtly testing if they are in a psychologically safe environment. If you are present, in the moment, and demonstrate that you are listening without judgment, then they may just build the courage to tell you what is "really" on their mind.

For example, you are having a one-on-one meeting with your team member, and you ask them what they would like to discuss today. They will very often start with relatively mundane updates before crescendoing to the thing that is most important to them. If you ever record and playback a conversation (not typically advisable by the way) you will find that in those opening statements the most important topic was the last thing they said. They are trying to get a read from you prior to that to see if you are ready for the "meaty" topic, or it could be just that they are building up the courage.

This is one to keep an eye on and see if you can determine patterns of speech and communication in people that you most often communicate with. One of the biggest signs that there is something troubling someone is behavior or speech that is "out of character" (the extrovert that becomes quiet, the calm person that becomes agitated). The more you observe your team's natural state the more tuned in you will be to anything out of the norm.

This is a skill that takes practice. Start by observing body language, facial expressions, and tone of voice. Listen without judgment and give the person the space to expand and share what is on their mind. With each conversation, you will be building a deeper understanding of that person. You may even wish to record notes in your self-reflection journal in the section titled "What I learned about others today."

The Power of the Pause (in 1:1 or group conversations)

There is a term called "awkward silence," and it is called that for a reason. Human beings do find silence in a conversation to be an awkward thing. You can use this to full effect as a leader and a communicator. Similar to the point above, it may take a little time for the other person to warm up and trust that they can open up the discussion to the thing that is most troubling them at this very moment.

By using deliberate pauses and silence you may well find that the other person fills the awkward gap. They get that little bit of discomfort with the silence and they open up with what is really on their mind. I have used this technique countless times and it continues to surprise me that the most insightful sharing normally comes after one of these awkward moments in the conversation.

The period of silence, particularly after a well-worded open question, can put the person into a reflective state. This enables them to discover things about themselves as they share with you. This reflective state can be transformative for their perception of the world and unlock new ways of thinking.

The Power of "Tell me more"

If you are also picking up (from body language or facial expression) that there is something bothering the other person and they just aren't completely opening up you can also use the powerful phrase, "Tell me more." This gives the other person the feeling that you are genuinely listening and interested in what they have to say and gives them the psychologically safe environment and license to be able to expand on their initial point.

If you go into a true coaching mindset, you may also go further with questions that expand the person's mind. For example, "What makes xxxx important to you?" (Helps one to understand significance.) Or "When you say xxxxx, what does xxxxx mean to you?" (Helps to ensure understanding of each other and avoiding assumptions.)

A good leader asks more questions than they provide answers. A great leader asks great questions. Open questions that expand the mind of the person they are talking with. Expansive questions that uncover significance and understanding for both you and that person. This puts them into a powerful reflective state where great learning can occur.

Try putting this into practice, and you will see surprising results.

Deep Listening and Theory U

One of my greatest mentors, Millar Crawford, is famous for saying, "you have two ears and one mouth, use them in that proportion." This is his beautiful way of saying that all communication starts with listening, and we should listen far more than we speak.

To take that to a new level I would like you to consider the work of Otto Scharmer of MIT in the development of Theory U and the practice of Deep Listening [18].

Pay close attention to this, there is something here for all of us.

In his groundbreaking work, Scharmer describes four levels of listening, and if you can master this, you will not only be able to become a greater listener and build deeper levels of connection with the people you are communicating with, you will also unlock greater levels of creativity in everything you and your team do.

Level 1 - Only listening to what you already know (or only listening to what you WANT to hear) - Most people live here. I am sure you have experienced this yourself. Either catching yourself doing it or seeing it in others. This manifests itself in multiple ways including:

- Only listening to things that confirm what you already know or believe.
- Listening to things that affirm a preconceived idea you had before the meeting even started (positive or negative).
- Not hearing the things that do not support your view or argument.
- Listening for what you want to hear and not hearing the things you don't want to hear (subconscious or conscious selective hearing) - I think we are all guilty of this at some point

To move past Level 1, you need to be ready to let go of what you think you already know. Go into a conversation with a learning mindset. Ready to learn new things, not with the objective of just proving to yourself (or others) how smart you are.

Level 2 - Listening with an Open Mind. Level 2 is keeping an Open Mind to new ideas, viewpoints, and concepts. To quote Mark Cole, CEO of the John C Maxwell group of companies, "Listen as if you know nothing." A key point to also listen for here is perspective. When someone else is expressing their view, it is from their vantage point and perspective and for them this perception is their reality. Cognitive Empathy will help put yourself in their shoes and see understand things from their vantage point. When someone is saying something that doesn't seem right from your perspective, try this pivot first and see it from their angle before commenting on your perspective and viewpoint.

"Seek first to understand, then to be understood. ® "
– Dr. Stephen R. Covey (The 7 Habits of Highly Effective People
®) (19)

Keeping an open mind is the only way to truly learn something new, and I am learning new things every day.

Diversity of thought is also a key attribute here. When listening with an open mind, we collect ideas from people with diverse backgrounds. People that have had different experiences to you. People that have different perspectives. When you bring these diverse thoughts together and bring them to the open everyone becomes richer from that experience. You and your team will find a better answer by being open to all of these perspectives, experiences, and viewpoints.

Level 3 - Listening with an Open Heart - Having an Open Heart means being open and listening to the emotion of the situation and of what is being said. You need to tap into the emotive driver of why someone may be expressing their viewpoint to get to a deeper level understanding of what they are trying to say.

Establishing that emotional connection will take all of your communication to the next level. The person you are communicating with will not only feel they are valued and they matter, they will also consider that you "get them."

Listening to emotion will also help you unlock one of the greatest lessons I have ever learned. It took me many years to learn this. As an engineer, I have always tried to make rational sense of the world and "how" things work. Therefore, whenever I was talking with someone, I was also looking for it to make sense, and I would get confused when someone would say something that was "irrational" even after taking into perspective cognitive empathy and trying to see things from their unique perspective. The summary is that human beings are generally emotional creatures and emotions drive the majority of our decisions.

Therefore, when someone does something seemingly "irrational," always remember that if it does seem irrational it is because it is *not* rational, it is *emotional.* Getting past this realization will help you greatly in your communication and listening and will help you rationalize an irrational world.

The first step is to "notice and name" when these emotional realizations occur. Reflect on them. It is always a good idea to confirm what you are noticing with that person. This can be done through powerful open questions like "How does that make you feel when you describe that situation?" It can also be to be clear about what you noticed with questions like "I noticed a shift in your body language just now; what is emerging for you here?" It is better to let them express it than to pre-suppose the answer. However, if they do not notice it themselves, you may need to do some prompting. For example "you seem to have a weight lifted off your shoulders there; what are you noticing?"

Level 4 - Listening with an Open Will - Not surprisingly, the final level is most certainly the hardest. Having an open will is to let go of your existing reality and imagine new possibilities and a new reality. This is also where great creativity can be unlocked in your team. An Open Will is where invention and innovation can reign supreme. Leave behind any thoughts of what you believe is a universal truth and imagine something new and beyond. If it wasn't for people with an Open Will we would all still think the world is flat, air travel would certainly not be possible, and we would still think it impossible for a human to run a mile in under four minutes or their heart would explode (for most of us that is still true).

Some exercises you can use here include the use of visualization and/or powerful questions. Get your team to consider and articulate beliefs that they once held as true that later proved to be not. A visualization may be prompted by asking "What would this look like if you remove all barriers and constraints such as time, budget, and resources?" An exploratory path could be unlocked by asking questions like, "What would need to be true for this to work?"

At Level 4, we enter the world of co-creation. When people are able to truly listen to each other with an Open Will, they can co-create something that is greater than the sum of the parts that were brought to the table. Holding space for each to expand our minds and discover something new from our collective experiences.

For more information on the power of deep listening, I highly recommend Don Campbell's book titled *Creativity: It's not what you think* [20]. Campbell's title is purposefully double meaning: creativity is not what you think it is, and it is not what you think. Well worth a read. Otto Scharmer has multiple books on Theory U that then take this concept to a whole new level if you are looking to delve deeper into this.

Active Listening and Filtering

These two topics are different, but I have coupled them together, and they complement each other very well.

When talking, everyone wants to feel they are being heard and that their opinions matter. This is where active listening comes in. Active listening is the process of showing the person that you are truly listening to them, and that you understand what they are saying.

To be clear, this does not have to mean that you agree with them, but that you have truly heard and understood them. This will be both through verbal acknowledgements that you hear and understand them and through your body language.

Verbal acknowledgements may be as simple as saying something like "I see" or "Go on" or "Tell me more."

Body language cues are critical in showing that you are being mindful and in the moment. Make the person feel that this conversation with them is the most important thing you can be doing right now. That you are here with them and no one else and that they have your undivided attention. Making appropriate eye contact is probably the most important, facing the person, and not being distracted by other things in your surroundings. There is something deeply disrespectful about someone checking their smartphone during a conversation or giving other signals that they are not completely there with you.

To really bring this point home for you, I want you to consider times where you have been in a conversation with someone and you know that they are not completely with you. They may be checking their phone or distracted by other things. They may even say things to you that demonstrate that they didn't hear what you just said. Now, think about how that made you feel at that moment. It does not feel good, does it? You feel unimportant at best or completely frustrated and maybe even angry.

Now, stop and reflect. Do you sometimes do the same? I certainly know that I have been guilty of this (and sometimes still do). Distracted by a message on my phone or watch, having a conversation but also having one eye on the rugby or tennis on the TV in the background, or even being in this conversation but my mind is busily thinking about something else that is playing on my mind. I am human; I make mistakes, but this is something that I am consciously working on every day to be a better listener, a better communicator, and to treat people with respect.

There are times in your life where needing to check your phone is critical (waiting on an urgent and time-critical call or message, etc.), but this is not usually the case. When this situation does arise, bring this up at the very start of the conversation and apologize and explain in advance.

A perfect example of this happened with me yesterday. I was having a great and meaningful conversation with Ian Westmoreland of Mentoring Men, a wonderful organization in Australia that supports men in their life journey and provides mentoring when they most need it. Ian was on-call to be the overflow if calls to their toll-free number exceeded the number of available mentors and he let me know this at the very start of the call. So, when a call came in, Ian was able to politely excuse himself to take the call, and both of us instantly knew that the call coming in was more important than what we were discussing.

You can extrapolate this to other examples in your own life and make your own judgments as to when this is appropriate and when it is not. Just be open with the other person and tell them in advance, "I am really sorry, but I will need to have my phone handy today because I am expecting a call from my son's school," etc.

This also raises a question about how to manage your body language, eye contact, and showing that you are in the moment, in a work-from-home world. At the time of writing this book, we are in the midst of the COVID-19 pandemic and people are taking more virtual meetings than anything else. The key here is that the same rules apply. People will soon be able to tell if you are not with them and in the moment. If you are on your phone, busy multitasking, or otherwise distracted. It is very easy to tell and just as disrespectful as if you were there in person.

One of the great leaders listed in my Amalgam Leader, Jeff Lowinger President of Cubic Transportation Systems, is exceptional at engaging on Zoom. He leaves you with no doubt that he is completely there with you and not distracted on other things. I have been quietly taking lessons from him on how he achieves this.

Some practical tips on managing engaging conversations in the virtual world:

1. Have your camera on.
2. Setup your camera:
   o with the lens at your normal eye level
   o as close as possible to where the person's face is on your Zoom screen
3. Alternate between looking at the person (so you can see their body language and facial expressions) and looking directly down the lens of

the camera (this does not always feel natural and may take some practice).

4. Put your phone out of reach so you can't be distracted by it.

5. Close or minimize other applications so you just have Zoom (or your preferred web conference) application on your screen.

6. Make sure that your eyes are not bouncing all over the place where people will just assume that you are reading something, typing something, or otherwise not fully in the moment.

7. Manage your calendar so that you are not working on other things at the time of that meeting.

8. Try scheduling meetings for 25 minutes or 55 minutes to give yourself a break before you move on to your next meeting or next task.

As you work on your active listening, there are some key points to observe:

- Tap into your own feelings about what it is like when someone gives you their full undivided attention. Remember what it feels like when you believe the other person is not really "there" with you.

- Listening is not the same as waiting for your turn to talk. Take the time, give them respect, and show that you care about what they are saying. As Teddy Roosevelt put it, "No one cares what you know, until they know how much you care."

- Be mindful, in the moment, and listen without judgment.

- As a leader, be really careful not to show signals too early about what you agree with and what you do not agree with. People will always be looking for signals about what is pleasing you, and you may unintentionally steer the direction of the conversation away from a new discovery or a completely open exchange of ideas.

Active listening is the ability to show someone that you are intently and attentively listening by reflecting back what you have heard them say, but to do so in your own words and to do so without judgment. Remember, you are just trying to show them that you have heard them at this stage, not passing any judgment on whether you agree, disagree, or otherwise. Using your own words to paraphrase back is also a wonderful way to check common understanding. Rather than repeat back verbatim if you put in your own words the person will have the ability to say, "Oh, that's not quite what I meant," and you can then go deeper to ensure you did indeed understand their message.

Filtering

The practice of filtering takes deliberate practice. When someone speaks they provide a lot of filler and an amount of context (sometimes that context is important, but not always). The human brain can only remember and focus on a certain number of things at any given time. Filtering is the ability to listen to complete paragraphs of information and to select the most important one to three things you have just heard. Listening to emotion in the language used, the use of adjectives and adverbs, and paying attention to body language will help you to filter out what is the "filler" and what is the true important substance of what the person is trying to say. The key elements you are looking for relate to their emotions: What are they feeling? What are they thinking? What is troubling them? Once you identify this key points you can summarize back to them to ensure that you identified the key elements. If you miss the mark they will normally tell you.

In the event you are unable to filter and sift through all of the things they are saying, you can bring focus to the conversation by asking questions like, "So what would you say is the real challenge for you here?"

As you build this filtering skill, you will find a deeper connection with people. They will feel that you have not just listened, but that you have really heard and understood what is more important to them.

The Power of the Summary (in meetings)

To build directly on the back of this filtering concept, this is also super helpful in meetings. Great leaders have a wonderful ability to listen to complex conversations among multiple people and to be able to sift through and find the most important points from the discussion. Chris Jenkins, CEO of Thales Australia, is a master at this, and so is Tom Walker, Managing Director of Cubic Asia Pacific.

Always remember that people will only take away a certain number of things from any meeting and you want them to remember the things that were most important. So, take the lead on this one and provide a short and succinct summary at the end of a meeting. If the meeting is particularly long and has multiple sections, you may need to do this summary at multiple stages.

If you are bold, you may even wish someone in the meeting to do the summarizing to build further ownership of the outcome. You could ask one of your potential successors to take this role.

This can also be a great technique to use if you have someone in the room that may be a little hesitant or resistant to the subject of this meeting. Getting them to summarize the outcomes builds their buy-in and it becomes difficult for them not to be on board if they were the ones summarizing.

This technique is also a wonderful superpower in a negotiation setting. Each time you have a breakthrough moment in a negotiation you want to summarize it straight away. This has the result of "locking in" that agreement before you move on to the next topic.

The 6Cs of Communication.

I had the great pleasure on The Leadership Project podcast to interview Lisa Partridge, the Founder of SIXCOMMS. Lisa is an expert in instructional design with a specialization in communication, facilitation, and presentation skills.

Lisa has helped some iconic organizations to improve the communication and presentation skills of their staff. This has included training for the world class cabin crew of Singapore Airlines, without any doubt the best airline in the world for customer service. She has also helped fast growing companies like TikTok and exceptional organizations like Marina Bay Sands.

Lisa has codified the keys to communication into 6Cs as follows:

- Clarity
- Connection
- Compassion
- Curiosity
- Customisation
- Consistency

I feel that she is spot on here. The 6Cs of communication could be applied in any context, but I do believe that they are very well suited to a Leadership context.

Moment of self-reflection

Take a moment now to stop, think, and reflect on your own communication style:

1. Think of the more impactful communicators you have experienced in your life and career?
2. What was common about them?
3. Reflect on communicators that you did not like.
4. What was common about them?
5. Now consider your own communication style. Does it more closely resemble the impactful communicators or the others?
6. Do you make assumptions without testing them?
7. Do you suffer or benefit from the Law of Attraction?
8. Do you pay attention to multi-sensory communication of others and of yourself?
9. Are you mindful and in the moment?
10. How would you describe your own listening skills?
11. Do you actively listen?
12. Do you deeply listen?
13. Do you listen without judgment?
14. Do you seek first to understand then to be understood? Or are you just waiting for your turn to speak?
15. What can you put into practice around powerful presentations and speeches? Around storytelling, emotion, the rule of 3s, deliberate use of pauses, and less is more?

Chapter Fourteen

Delivering Powerful Presentations and Speeches

Delivering speeches and presentations

Before long in your career as a leader, you will almost certainly be called upon to deliver impactful presentations and/or speeches. This could be representing your organization at an external event such as a customer meeting or conference or it could be an internal meeting with your team or with senior management.

For internal presentations, this may include giving updates on the direction of the organization or presenting new ideas, concepts, and initiatives. In all cases, presentations to your team should stick to the Leader's wheelhouse of inspiring people into action and making them feel part of the solution and not just that they are being spoken to.

For management presentations, customer presentations, or conferences, these may be status updates, but nearly always will involve convincing someone of a certain argument or direction you would like to head.

Delivering powerful presentations can become a complex topic and one that could warrant a future book. For this book, I am just going to break down the three most impactful lessons I have learned in my career about what works.

If you put these three things into action, I guarantee that your presentations will improve and be significantly more impactful.

The Power of Emotion

Stories connect and persuade us almost more than anything else. A powerful story enables something inside of us. Something where we see ourselves in that situation and feel the emotions that the protagonist in the story feels. Stories are generally more memorable than facts and figures or rational thought as they play to our emotions.

The key to any memorable speech or presentation is emotion. Specifically, it is the emotion that the audience experiences and how you make them feel.

In preparing for any presentation or speech, this is the perfect place to start. Ask yourself the question, "What emotions do I want the audience to feel during this presentation?" After this, you can start thinking about what your key messages will be. It is okay to do it the other way around, but do not forget the importance of emotion if you really want your speech (and its content) to be memorable.

To unlock that emotion, you do need to understand who your audience is. Empathize with who they are, what their challenges may be, and then meet them where they are. A key aspect to be careful of is assumed knowledge. As you develop more and more expertise in your field, it becomes more difficult to remember that not everyone knows what you already know, making it a danger to go complex when you should be sticking to the basics and first principles. Once you have empathized with your audience, start thinking about how you want them to be transformed by your speech at its conclusion. What did you want them to feel, and what do you want them to take away at the end?

Pay close attention to ensure that your story is:

- Simple
- Organized
- Relatable

As Einstein famously said, the art is to "make it as simple as possible (but no simpler)" to get your point across.

Always remember that not everyone in your audience has the same level of mastery of the English language. Make sure that the story is organized and structured in a way that they can follow but also captures and retains their attention.

Start with a strong opening that builds intrigue and ensure your closing reverts back to how you opened the story. To ensure the audience feels emotion, ensure that the story is relatable to them. Something where they can picture themselves in that story.

There are multiple ways to get people to feel emotion in your speech. The three most common ways are:

- **Express that emotion yourself (or in your imagery)**. Let yourself go, be vulnerable, and do not be afraid to show that emotion. If a topic gets you fired up, get fired up. If something makes you angry, get angry (to a degree), if something makes you sad don't be afraid to show it. Expressing this emotion can be as simple as saying it, but is far more powerful if they can see it in your facial expressions, body language, and tone of voice. When using this technique, always make sure that the emotion expressed is consistent with the message, do not over exaggerate it, and always make sure it is authentic. People will see straight through it if you are acting.

1. The alternative to expressing the emotion yourself (which can be confronting) is to use imagery in your presentation that evokes that emotion. The use of less data or bullet points and more imagery is a great way to get people to feel emotion and to remember your presentation later.

o **Ask probing questions.** Ask the audience open questions about how the situation makes them feel. Even if they are rhetorical questions delivered with deliberate pauses. Get the audience to stop and think. If you can get the audience in a reflective mindset it is almost impossible for them not to feel some level of emotion.

- **The art of storytelling.** This is well documented, and I am sure that you have experienced this yourself. When you walk away from the speech or presentation, if the presenter was a powerful storyteller you will remember that story forever. Even if you don't remember every single detail of the story, you will remember the outline, you will remember the lesson (or moral) of that story, and you will remember the emotion you felt. There are a number of great resources on YouTube and the internet on how to embrace storytelling in your presentations and speeches. It is

151

not as difficult as you think and often getting past the hurdle of getting started is one of the more challenging parts. Once you get started it does start to flow for you. Of course, it absolutely does require practice and you will get better at it the more you do it.

The Rule of Threes

When you study the speech patterns of some of the greatest orators throughout time, a clear and repeatable pattern emerges. For whatever reason, speech patterns always seem to be more impactful in groups of threes. Study great speeches and prose from William Shakespeare, John F. Kennedy, Barack Obama, Martin Luther King, Nelson Mandela, Winston Churchill, Abraham Lincoln, and all have all mastered this principle in their memorable speeches.

Think of examples like:

- "Friends, Romans, Countrymen..." - William Shakespeare
- "I came, I saw, I conquered." - Julius Caesar
- "Government of the people, by the people, for the people." - Abraham Lincoln

These are all examples of the Rule of 3s in short form. It also can be used in longer form. The key is the pattern and rhythm with each of the three being of the same or similar length.

Often it can even be three identical words or with identical meaning that when put in the Rule of 3s makes it more memorable. For example, the number one rule of real estate is "location, location, location."

When you look around you will start seeing it everywhere:

- Ready, aim, fire
- Ready, set, go
- ABC
- Faster, stronger, higher
- Father, Son, and The Holy Ghost

- Bacon, lettuce, and tomato
- Tom, Dick, and Harry
- Up, up, and away
- Lights, camera, action

Here is an example of how I have used the Rule of 3s for great effect. When discussing my vision for the world of mobility I often use this phrase "We will create a world where people can move freely around their cities—without congestion, without delays, without stress." This has never failed to resonate with audiences.

The Rule of 3s can be further accentuated combined with alliteration. Some great examples include:

- "Slip, Slop, Slap" - a famous Australian campaign for protection against sun cancer
- "See something, say something, solve something"
- "going, going, gone"

Alliteration can also be powerful without the Rule of 3s as well. For example, the motto of The Leadership Project is "Lead Together, Learn Together."

The power of pauses in speech

The power of using pauses in your speech patterns cannot be understated or underestimated. Experts at this phenomenon include Barack Obama, John C. Maxwell, and Simon Sinek—all master orators who captivate their audiences.

The key is to insert a deliberate and noticeable pause immediately before and after key points and phrases in your speech.

The science behind this is that it works for multiple reasons and on multiple levels as follows:

1. **Maintaining (or regaining) your audience's full attention**. It is really difficult for humans to provide undivided attention at all times

(as much as we try). So if you are delivering a presentation or speech of longer than two to three minutes, there will be moments where the audience members' minds may drift on to other thoughts and your voice becomes the background instead of their focus. By deliberately pausing and creating silence, something happens where the people will divert their attention back to you to see what happened. You now have their undivided attention at the most important point you are trying to make.

2. **Delayed Processing.** Most people take time to process new information. If you have just said something critical, important, and profound, you want to give people time to process that information before saying anything else. When processing, they will be trying to understand that statement, trying to relate it themselves, and trying to see if it resonates with them. If you immediately continue without a pause, one of two things will happen:

   o They will still be thinking about what you just said and will not hear your next point, or
   o They will be listening to your next point and will not have processed what you just said. If they don't process and relate to the important statement you just made, they will almost certainly not remember it.

3. **Language and Translation.** In an increasingly international, global, and multicultural world, you will more often than not be presenting to people that do not share the same level of proficiency of language and/or have the same native tongue. I have the deepest respect for multilingual people. People that can easily keep up with concurrent conversations in multiple languages. However, most of us are not like that. For me, my native tongue is (Australian) English, and I speak basic to intermediate French. I can listen to speeches in French and pick up nearly everything that is said. That is, until the person speaks too fast and without pauses. Then I am lost and I start feeling left out and anxious. Now, let's put the shoe on the other foot. Picture that I am delivering a speech in English and the people in my audience are

French, Cantonese, Chinese, Thai, Spanish, etc., where English is not their native language. There may even be native English speakers that are struggling with my Australian accent (which is not strong compared to some, but nonetheless is there). Now, if I speak too fast, without pauses, and without emphasis, I am almost certainly going to lose them at some point and lose the impact of the presentation that I have prepared long and hard for.

4. This has led me to a reminder I use before every presentation I give. "Remember, Mick, at least half of your audience may not speak English as their first language, and the other half may struggle to understand your accent."

I have a great story to illustrate this. Two very good friends of mine, Neil George and Bob Langridge, were on a business trip together to France. On day one of the trip, Bob was delivering a presentation to a mostly French audience. All were fluent in English, but French was their native language. Bob started his presentation with his thick Australian accent, speaking at a normal speaking pace. After a period of seven to eight minutes, Neil overheard one of the French team say, "Oh, he is speaking English." Now, this is an extreme case, but I hope that it clearly illustrates the point. Bob was speaking too fast and it took time for the audience to even process what language he was speaking.

Overuse of idioms

Another common trap to fall into is the overuse of idioms. Every language has them, and they often do not translate well into other languages. In Bob's natural speech, he will often use Australian idioms, expressions and even social references that other Australians (and perhaps Kiwis) would understand but would be completely lost on others.

Once again to illustrate the point I will use the opposite sense. The French language is also full of idioms that non-French native speakers would be completely befuddled with. Even if they are able to translate the words, the meaning would be lost.

Some quick examples: The French idiom "couter les yeux de la tête." The literal translation is "costs the eyes in your head.. This could be interpreted in so many ways, but really it just means the price is too expensive. The closest equivalent in English would be "costs an arm and a leg," which is obviously also not literal.

Another example is "tomber la chemise." The literal translation is take off your shirt, but before anyone starts disrobing, it just means "relax" and usually is in the context of being at the end of a long day of tiring work.

Less is More and The Dilutive Effect

Once again, here are two different topics, but they do go hand in hand. One of the greatest mistakes people make when presenting is to try to present every single thing they know into that one presentation, or worst still, everything on a topic on one slide.

The simple things to remember here are:

- **People will only remember three to five things from your presentation or speech.** By including 30+ items (as many people do), you are leaving it to chance which of the 30+ messages they are going to remember (if any when you consider overload). By reducing your presentation to the most important three to five messages, you are now in control of what they take away and remember from you.

- **Busy slides, busy mind.** If you build slides that better resemble an eye chart at the optometrist, you now have no control over what the audience is focusing on. You may be saying the most insightful things, but if they are busy reading every word on your chart, then you are not influencing their focus, and you have lost them somewhere along the way. By reducing your chart to a single statement, or better yet a simple emotive image, you will be able to maintain their focus and have their undivided attention. A practical tip on this: When I am saying the single most important part of my presentation, I will often completely blank the screen and draw the attention back to what I am saying at that moment.

- **The Dilutive Effect.** When formulating an argument to proceed with a certain action (buy your product, approve a business case, etc.) people often think that the more arguments they put forward, the more compelling their argument is. "How can the boss possibly say no, I have 16 reasons why we should do this?" Though this may seem counterintuitive to many, you are far better off with three compelling reasons than to keep on adding on top. There are two reasons for this. Firstly, the dilutive effect means that with every additional argument you add to your list, you are actually diminishing the importance of the arguments you have already presented. You may well have already convinced your audience after three, but those three reasons are now lost in a sea of information where people can no longer distinguish between what was really important and what was just an "added bonus." When you had three reasons they were most likely weighing those factors in their head, perhaps not evenly 33/33/33, but perhaps 50/30/20 in their importance. Once you get to 16 reasons (as mentioned above) you are now looking at each reason potentially only carrying 6.25 percent of the load.

1. The second reason is that with each additional argument you put forward you run the risk that something in one of your statements is not 100 percent accurate and someone in the audience picks up on it. Your presentation has now turned into a conversation about that topic (which was probably minor) instead focusing on the three compelling reasons why your proposal should proceed.

The conclusion here is to do your homework, build the trust in the audience that you have done your homework, and then just present the most compelling three to five messages.

The Power of Storytelling

Another great skill for a great leader to have is the ability to use metaphors and the ability to tell engaging stories to their teams that inspire them to stop, think, and reflect. The story needs to capture their attention and imagination, but always have a reason for that story.

The most powerful stories enable visualization and evoke emotion from the recipient to make them even more memorable.

One of my great mentors, Millar Crawford, is the undisputed master of this. He has the amazing ability to stop a conversation with an outlandish statement that makes everything stop and think what on earth is he talking about. However, he always had the skill perfected that you couldn't ignore that statement and you knew that the story was always going to lead to something for us all to learn from. With the way the story was told, and with the bonus of a wonderful Northern Irish accent, the story (and lesson) would be remembered forever.

My all-time favorite statement was "But who's going to get the dog?" The context was in relation to our engagement with new customers in the business and the tendency to start overthinking before we have even started the conversation with them. The short version goes something like this:

"But who's going to get the dog?" Imagine you are on the dating scene, and your customer is at a bar, and you find them attractive and think they may be just your type. Before walking up to them at the bar, you start playing out the entire relationship in your head. You imagine success. You may have a few drinks together, dance the night away, and have a great time. Over the coming weeks, you continue to go on dates and have a wonderful time, and before you know it, you start to fall in love. You move in together, start sharing everything together, you take the big step of adopting a dog as a pet, and you may even get married. Then the seeds of doubt creep in and you start wondering about ALL of the things that could go wrong. What if we fall out of love? What if we have disagreements? What if it is not all smooth sailing? You start thinking of all the ways you might need to protect yourself from hurt and pain. Despite the reservations, you pick up the courage and go over to talk to your customer, and when you open your mouth instead

of starting with "Hi, what is your name?" You open with "But who's going to get the dog?"

I am not saying that every leader needs to become a master storyteller to the same degree as Millar, but what I do encourage you to do is explore how you can embrace storytelling as one tool in your toolkit. When you think there comes a moment where you believe there is an important life or business lesson to share with your team, consider how you could frame that lesson into a story. If it is a really important lesson that you want them to remember, this is a great way to make it unforgettable.

A key point of powerful storytelling is keeping the story simple, organized, and relatable to the audience. Use simple language, use structure in the story as much as possible, and ensure that you use real life references that everyone will relate to.

I would say it is also important to not use this as your first approach in any given situation. Always remember that people tend to learn more through a journey of self-discovery than being "told" something. So, if you can draw the lesson out of the team, this will be more powerful.

Also, do not overuse this technique. If you use it every single time it may lose some of its effect and the team may start feeling "Oh, here we go again, more stories."

A moment of self-reflection

Consider now the following questions:

1. Have you had leaders in your career, like Millar, that were able to use storytelling to share lessons with you and your team?
2. How did those stories make you feel?
3. To what degree did the leader capture your attention?
4. How did they use emotion and emotive queues in their story?
5. How did they bring the story to a conclusion with the lesson?
6. Do you still remember that story and lesson today?
7. How could you start to practice using storytelling in your leadership toolkit?
8. Consider the greatest speeches and presentations you have sat through
9. What was common about them?
10. Consider the least impactful presentations you have sat through?
11. What was common about them?
12. Do you use simple, organized, and relatable structure and storytelling?
13. Do you embrace the power of 3s?
14. Do you use pauses for emphasis?
15. Could you replace "um" and "ah" with pauses?
16. Are you careful with the overuse of idioms?
17. Do you embrace the "less is more" principle and avoid the "dilutive effect?"

Chapter Fifteen

Conversational Intelligence

Conversational Intelligence is a very complex topic in its own right with many resources in which you can study this further. I highly recommend the work of the late Judith Glaser who was a pioneer in this field.

However, without going into depth on this topic, there are some basics that all leaders should consider in the language they use and the way they speak. This chapter will cover some useful tips that leaders should follow and address some phrases they are often misinterpreted if you are not careful.

The language of "we" vs "I"

A common trait of great leaders is they often talk in the collective and the world of co-creation. They will emphasize this with the word "we" instead of "I," and they will do so in almost all settings. The two exceptions are they will use the word "I" when expressing personal emotions and when taking personal accountability for performance or mistakes. In doing so, stepping up to protect the team. They will revert back to "we" when acknowledging successes and ensuring the spotlight shines on the team.

Great leaders always know and acknowledge that it is not about them, but about their team. The key here is the choice of language to ensure that their team feels that they are an important part of something bigger and that the work they do matters.

The opposite is when the team feels that the leader is constantly taking credit for the work of the broader team and they do not feel acknowledged for their contribution to success.

In summary, be careful with your language. It is not about you, it is about your team.

Other words and language to be careful with

Actually - "Actually, that is a great idea." This is often used with heavy emphasis and intonation that signals surprise. When people use this it can be interpreted as "That is a great idea; I am just surprised that it came from you." As you can imagine this is highly demotivating and disrespectful. The simple tip here is to just omit it. Have a look at most sentences where "actually" is used and the sentence would *actually* still make sense if the word was removed (pun intended).

Just - The word "just" diminishes the importance of the next words you say next. Examples include "I am just writing to you to see if…" or "I just want five minutes of your time." This is another candidate where omitting the word "just" is the simplest remedy. Most sentences would stand complete with the word "just" removed.

Very, absolutely, and totally are words that are typically superfluous to any sentence. An exercise you can try is to read your sentence back without these words and see if it still makes sense without them. *(Note: I am acutely aware I use the word "very" far too often so I will not be surprised if it appears multiple times in this book, unless my wonderful editors Allison and Qat have already removed them :-))*

Try - "Do or do not; there is no try." - Master Yoda. The words "I'll try" signal that you are uncertain in your abilities and reduces the confidence of your team that you will follow through with what you promise. I would encourage you to remove the word from your vocabulary and encourage your team to do the same

Honestly signals that other things you have said may have been false. For example, "I honestly feel this is the right way to go" does signal that you believe in the current path, but brings into some doubt that you have not always felt that way about other decisions and directions. You can look to omit "honestly" altogether, or you can replace it with terms like "I feel strongly that this is the right course of action" if you want to emphasize your support.

Don't Worry - Using the words "Don't worry" does the opposite; it *makes* people worry and makes them feel less valued. If they weren't worried already, they may well be after you raise worry into the conversation. Additionally, asking someone not to worry can signal that it is not "for them" to worry about. This is dismissive and signals that you believe this problem is beyond their capabilities to understand or help with. This makes them feel they don't matter and feel excluded.

Obviously can make other people feel stupid. It might be obvious to you, but may not have been obvious to them. Something may have been very obvious to you from your experience but not everyone in the world shares that same experience you have had.

Yes, but... - Whenever you use "Yes, but..." you are sending mixed signals. You are agreeing with the person by saying "Yes" and then immediately negating that with your "but" statement. Rather than using "Yes, but..." replace it with "Yes, and..." This is now an additive statement that values that person's input and then builds upon it with additional information, context, and ideas. The use of "Yes, and..." is used widely in improvised comedy and is very useful during brainstorming, problem solving, and ideation sessions. It is an empowering and enabling statement for all involved and encourages others to also contribute their ideas because they are not going to be shot down with a "but" statement.

The power of "**yet**" and "**used to.**" These are powerful and positive words that you can add to your vocabulary. This is another powerful lesson I have taken from Chandler Bolt of Self-Publishing School. He makes a practice of adding these words to turn a negative into a positive frame: future, past, or present. For example, if someone asks Chandler "Have you met Barack Obama?" he will answer "Oh no, I haven't met him **yet**." *(Note: I am not sure if Chandler has or has not met President Obama **yet**. I will have to ask him).* He will also employ the words "used to" in a positive frame as well. Instead of someone saying "I am not good at writing" he would encourage them to reframe it as "I used to not be good at writing" to help put their imposter syndrome behind them.

Moment of self-reflection

Take some moments now to stop, think, and reflect on the language that you use with your team and whether it is constructive or destructive.

Considering the following questions over the coming days:

1. Are there any phrases that you hear other people use that "get under your skin" or make you feel less valued?
2. Are there phrases that others use that you think can be open to misinterpretation in comparison to the intended meaning?
3. Do you notice the reactions of others when they hear these phrases?
4. Now, reflect on yourself. Do you find yourself using any of these same phrases?
5. What could you replace them with?

Chapter Sixteen

High-Performance Teams

In December, 2009 I was extremely honored to be appointed as the Global Project Director of the Auckland Integrated Fares System project for Thales. This came after a long and protracted tendering process that began in February 2008. I had been the bid manager for the tender submission, the customer presentations, and ensuing contract negotiations. This led to the point where I had built up considerable knowledge of the project, the contract, and the solution we were offering. In some respects I became an obvious candidate for the role, but in many respects this was a big jump in my career to go from a big manager through to directing a $150 million project with teams spread across the world. I owe a huge debt of gratitude to Pierre Maciejowski and Laurent Eskenazi for that leap of faith. They had seen my potential, my attitude, and my aptitude and backed my appointment and proceeded to develop, support, and mentor me through this.

This was a big turning point in my career with many lessons learned (positive and negative). This role and experience resulted in many of the values and beliefs that make me who I am today.

This project and experience also resulted in the development of some amazing friendships that will stay with me for life. Friendships with my fellow Thales team with people like Neil George, Gabriel Gonzales, Jane Bates, Stan Low, and Ross Nicol, to name just a few. Friendships with our close partner in Octopus with Brian Chambers, Nora Tang, and Ernest Wong. Friendships with customers like Steve Budd and Greg Ellis. All friendships that I will cherish for all time.

The development of these friendships and relationships begins my first understanding that leadership is all about how we relate to other people.

One of the biggest challenges facing this project was how we would manage to deliver such a complex undertaking with a team of circa 170 people (120 full-time staff plus functional part-time support) that were spread across four countries, time zones, and cultures. We had a large development team (hardware and software) in France, an amazing supplier in Hong Kong (Octopus), a small but formidable customer facing team in Auckland, NZ and a great support team in Australia.

With the great foresight of Kim Hall and David Morley, we got together to design an extensive project kick-off activity to bring this very diverse team together. At a considerable expense, we invested the time and money to bring the key leaders of this project to co-locate together in Hong Kong for four full days of team building and project launch.

With the exceptional facilitation of Ross Nicol we went through four days together mixing all of these cultures and people to decide just how we would execute this project, spent time bonding and getting to know each other, and conducted launch activities that would create a common project baseline (scope, schedule, budget, milestones, measures of success) that everyone understood and committed to.

We also took the bold step of inviting our customer's representative, Greg Ellis, to join us for these days to share what was most important to him in the execution of this project.

The team building was a mix of sometimes challenging and thought-provoking exercises and some things that were just pure fun.

Ross led us through some confronting exercises around personal preferences and getting to know each other on a very deep level. This built amazing empathy among the team. It built the realization that we are all different, we are all unique, we all have different working style preferences, but collectively we could achieve amazing things.

We also had some great fun along the way such as the "The Amazing Race - Hong Kong" where we broke up into cross-functional and cross-cultural teams in a race around Hong Kong, solving puzzles and riddles along the way, all the while using the Octopus card for everything we did. The Octopus Card is a single card that allows you to do many aspects of your daily life in Hong Kong. Everything from catching the bus or train through to buying coffee and getting access to buildings. This was particularly relevant as the project we were embarking on was going to bring a scheme similar to Octopus to the people of Auckland and we wanted to develop a deep level of customer empathy for what it takes to use such a system. One of the engineers even pulled me aside to say that this was the first time he had actually used one of our systems in live operations despite being in the industry for more than a decade. He truly appreciated the empathy and understanding that this brought to him.

All of these different exercises then culminated on day four with the development of our team charter, a document shared by all that captured how we would work together on the project. Spending the first three days working through different topics, getting to know each other, building empathy for each other and our customers led to the development of a team charter that was based on real substance. This resulted in a much richer and more valid team charter. I have been involved in other team charters in the past and without a shared experience and understanding of each other, the team charters can sometimes be built on generic statements rather than statements of specific substance.

The Team Charter addressed key aspects of how we would work together and be successful together as a team including our vision and mission, how we would communicate, how we would prioritize, how we would treat each other, and our shared values and beliefs about the project and about each other.

We developed a shared vision that the Hop card (a single card for accessing all public transport options) would become an everyday part of life for the people of Auckland. Something I am proud to say we truly achieved. We agreed on our values and beliefs and how we would treat and respect each other. We agreed on communication approaches including answering a key question: "How can we convert the time zone differences into an advantage rather than a challenge?" We agreed on how we would measure performance and reward and recognize our teams. We agreed on what success would look like. We agreed on responsibilities and accountabilities.

The most important thing we agreed on was that we would all live by that charter, including having the ability to "call each other on it" if someone was straying away from the values and beliefs in that charter.

There are certainly some negative lessons learned from this project, including the point about becoming a point of dependence for the team covered earlier in this book, but the team charter was one of great success. The investment that we made in time and money for those four days had an enormous return with regard to building the team and setting the course for project success. You could say that we dramatically accelerated the normal stages of team development from Forming, Storming, Norming, to Performing. The fact that over the course of the project we continually lived by the Charter showed the great success of those four days.

I will be eternally thankful to the team for the vision of Kim Hall and David Morley in setting that up and then the amazing facilitation and execution of from Ross Nicol as he expertly led us through this process.

Stages of Team Development

There are various models of team development for high-performance teams that all follow a relatively similar pattern with stages of development. A high-performance team is generally considered to be one where the collective power of the team far outweighs the impact of any one individual. Where the team has a defined vision and a common mission. Where everyone understands their role and contribution to team success. Where there is an element of healthy and defined co-dependence on each other to achieve amazing feats. Where you are able to co-create something that is far greater than the sum of the parts.

Tuckman's stages of team development describes a team that goes through the following phases:

1. Forming
2. Storming
3. Norming
4. Performing

In the Forming stage, the team members are really just getting to know each other, feeling each other out, and have no common direction or purpose.

In the Storming phase, you will start seeing an increase in clarity of purpose but will also see a lot of conflict and potentially some power struggles as team members are trying to find their place in the team.

In the Norming phase you will start seeing a lot more consensus and agreement on purpose and vision and there will be clearer roles and responsibilities for everyone on the team.

In the Performing phase, you will have complete clarity of vision and purpose and on the goals that are needed to achieve that vision. You will go beyond just having clear roles and responsibilities, you will see interdependencies being clearly understood and utilized to full effect. People go beyond knowing what their role is. They understand their role, they will understand everyone else's role, and they will understand how their role supports other team members and vice versa. Team members at this stage will understand that group success is dependent on each member performing their role and interacting and sharing with others. At this stage you have developed a team where the performance of the team is greater than the sum of its parts. There will typically be a deep level of trust and confidence amongst the team—trust for each other and trust in the leader. The team would have also developed a high level of resilience with the ability to flex and support each other in the event that one or more team members are having a moment where they need support. A high-performance team typically has a learning cycle of continuous self-improvement and is always looking to collectively sharpen performance.

Drexler-Sibbet Team Performance Model

The other model that I have had great success with is the Drexler-Sibbet Team Performance Model [21]. The Drexler-Sibbet model takes teams through the following stages:

1. Orientation - Why am I here?
2. Trust Building - Who are you?

3. Goal Clarification - What are we doing?

4. Commitment - How will we do it?

5. Implementation - Who does what, where, and when?

6. High Performance - When WOW happens!

7. Renewal - Why continue?

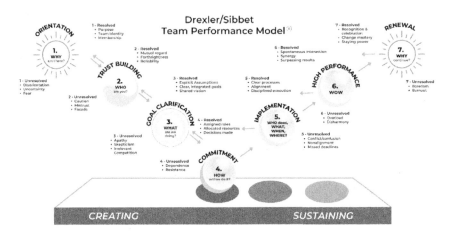

I particularly like in the Drexler-Sibbet model that it gives clear guidance on how to baseline the team, measure where you are at, and how to move the team from one phase to the next.

An interesting exercise you can do, at almost any stage in a team's life, is to print out a large chart of the Drexler-Sibbet model and put it on a wall in your conference room. You then give each team member a post-it note and allow them to post where they think the team is at. This builds collective team self-awareness. It enables a conversation on "what they would like to see happen?" to move the team along the continuum of performance. This can be super powerful to build engagement and ownership of the team's journey.

It is important to note that in any of these models, you cannot rest on your successes. There are a variety of reasons that can lead a team to take a backward step in the development phases. This could be external changes of circumstances, it could be the introduction of new team members or turnover, or it could be an internal event that eroded trust somewhere along the way.

This will mean that you may need to revisit some of these stages of development with perhaps the need to re-form, re-storm, or re-norm.

It is very common in team environments for cracks to perform in team harmony over time. It is at these moments it is powerful to reconduct exercises like Drexler-Sibbet to "reset" where the team is at.

There are occasions where bringing in an external facilitator or mediator may be required to help the team break down barriers to performance that may have emerged. A great and mature leader will embrace such an action and not see it as a threat but rather an opportunity to raise the team's performance back to higher levels.

Getting to know each other

A key driver in team performance is having a group of people that know, like, and trust each other. A key technique in driving this is to provide a platform and rituals that allow people to share their own story. This can be performed at any stage in the life of the team, but I encourage you to start early and do it often. Typically, this would start with the leader but should spread through the entire team. I have personally had great success, early in my time with a new team, to conduct a presentation talking about me. This might sound self-centered, but I regularly get supportive comments that this shows me as human and makes it clear about who I am and what I stand for. In this session I will share my personal why and vision including what drives me to get out of bed in the morning. I openly share what I believe my strengths and weaknesses are and show that I am human just like everyone else. I explain my personal preferences and personality traits, my likes, my dislikes, and share a little of my personal and professional history. I also share with the entire team my values and beliefs, my passions, and also the things that I have little tolerance for (in my case that is willful breaches of safety, any form of discrimination, and any form of harassment).

Following on from this, I then work through one team member at a time and give each a chance to present their own story, what makes them tick, and their own values, beliefs and preferences. This is conducted at each team meeting until every member has had their turn. Some will be nervous about it, but all will be appreciative of the opportunity to share their story, to feel heard, and to feel valued. This is a great way to introduce new hires and team members into the team environment. To quickly make them feel that they belong.

This process goes a long way to build empathy and understanding in the team and sets up the foundations for trust.

Shared Experience

A great way to accelerate team performance is to have the team go through some level of shared experience together. This can come in a myriad of forms, but could include team-building exercises (such as the Amazing Race - Hong Kong mentioned earlier), it could include doing charity work together, or working on a team project like putting a short video together.

A shared experience creates a memorable event that the team will talk about and reference for years to come.

Moment of self-reflection

Take the time now to stop, think, and reflect on teams you have been in before, or perhaps the team you are in now.

1. Where would you say that team fits on Tuckman's Stages of Development or on the Drexler-Sibbet Team Performance Model?
2. What events or circumstances led the team to be there?
3. What could you do to help the team move forward on those scales?
4. If they are already high performing, what will you do to maintain that?
5. What external or internal forces might lead you to revisit the team's performance stage?

Chapter Seventeen

Diversity

The Importance of Diversity

Standing on a stage right now somewhere in the world is a CEO speaking at a Town Hall meeting and "authoritatively" telling their staff about the company's drive for Diversity & Inclusion. They are probably showing graphs on gender balance and declaring a company target or KPI.

However, a key question is whether they truly understand what diversity and inclusion are and why they are important. Or are they just repeating what they have seen other CEOs doing? Or perhaps just delivering a speech written from someone in HR?

One of the most memorable moments (for the wrong reason) in my career came early in the resurgent push for diversity and inclusion in the workplace. The CEO of the company I was working for at the time was told that he had to address D&I in a speech to the staff. He proceeded to tell the entire congregation of staff that "Diversity and inclusion is about employing less-capable people." Shockingly, you could tell that he really believed that. However, the response from the gathered audience was a mixture of shock, dismay, and people murmuring statements like "that must be how you got your job."

If we are truly going to challenge the status quo and make a meaningful impact in the world, we need leaders that understand what diversity and inclusion is, why it is important, and take positive action to ensure diversity is embraced in their organizations. We don't need more rhetoric, we need more action.

So, how can you start?

As a leader, you can start making a difference early in your career. You can take the time to learn the importance of diversity and inclusion and to pass that knowledge on to your teams. You can reinforce the right behaviors, you can call out inequity, you can address immediately any behaviors that you see that are dismissive of that importance.

What is diversity?

Firstly, we need to say it is more than just a gender-balance issue. Diversity is about creating teams made up of people from diverse backgrounds and from all walks of life.

Beyond just gender, it includes a long list of attributes including age, religion, race, sexual orientation and preference, socioeconomic background, country of origin, school, educational background, single people, parents, profession, skillsets, extroverts, introverts, people with mobility issues, people with a variety of life experiences, and the list goes on.

For a specific industry there may be a need to have diversity across a specific spectrum. For example, having worked in Public Transport technology for a decade and a half I always found it valuable to have people that were transit dependent, transit by choice, cyclists, walkers, and car drivers on my teams.

Why is it important?

Diversity of thought

There are multiple reasons why diversity is so important. Top of that list for me is that it fosters diversity of thought. If you surround yourself with people that look like you and think like you, you will just end up with a group of people that agree with you at every turn and will not challenge your thinking or your blind spots (we all have them).

Our background, our experiences, our knowledge and skills coupled with our preferences make up a large chunk of who we are and how we think. Therefore, having diversity of these factors directly increases your team's ability to group think and problem solve.

When I first started at one specific multinational company, the entire executive committee of the organization consisted of white, middle-aged, male, engineers who all went to the same university and were educated by the same faculty of professors. This meant that when faced with any question or problem in the business (from growth strategy through to crisis management) there was a very high probability they would all approach the topic with a similar perspective. This also leads to a high probability of a lot of agreement and back slapping, congratulating themselves for doing a great job. Meanwhile, the organization suffers from a lack of diversity of thought, an inability to inspire creativity and innovation, and an uninspired workforce. Another critical factor is that this reinforces the glass ceiling. People that do not fit the mold of middle-aged white male engineer from a certain university have a clear indication that their career will be limited below a certain threshold. As time passes and the world matures, this is now being seen as a big factor as to whether you can attract and retain a diverse workforce in the first place. If you show no diversity on your board or at the executive level, talented people are going to look elsewhere to advance their careers.

Resilience

Another key reason to drive diversity is to build resilience in your teams. Having diverse backgrounds across team members will lead to having a variety of coping skills under different situations and stressors. A high-performance team will be greater than the sum of its parts and will have the ability to dynamically adjust and rally around each other when needed. When you have diversity in your team, there is an increased chance that when one of the team is going through a rough patch that someone else on the team has been there before and is well placed to help them when they need it the most.

Empathy

Having diversity in your team will also be an enabler for empathy for the customers and stakeholders you serve. This includes customers or end users of your products and services.

This is critical for innovation. Developing new products and services that are relevant to your target market is heavily reliant on having a deep level of customer empathy. Understanding your customers' needs, wants, pains, and gains. Understanding what they see, hear, sense, and feel leads to a much better product.

If you have a deeper level of diversity in your team there is a much greater chance of developing a deep level of customer empathy.

Diversity should not be an arbitrary number

One thing that diversity should not be is an arbitrary target or number. I respect the need to measure progress and improvement, but having an arbitrary target is not really the point. Of particular note, these arbitrary targets are usually just gender based and miss the multi-dimensional nature of diversity. I do encourage organizations to measure their progress, but would advise being careful not to set targets that stimulate unexpected outcomes and lose sight of why it is important in the first place. Your role as a leader here is to always remain focussed on why diversity is important rather than getting fixated on a number that you may have been asked to achieve.

Diversity across functional departments

Something that is sometimes lost in this discussion is the lack of diversity across functional departments. Organizations drive for gender diversity to meet their arbitrary target but end up with a skewed balance. Functions like finance, HR, marketing, communication, and administration end up with a high representation of females, and functional departments like engineering, sales, and IT remain male dominated.

The net result is having a lack of gender diversity inside teams. This is in both directions. Having a Finance or HR team that is dominated by females is just as detrimental as having a team of engineers that is exclusively male.

If you are going to attract and retain a diverse workforce and team, you need a deep understanding and empathy of the people you are trying to attract. An often-forgotten fact is that a job interview is a two-way process;

the applicants are assessing whether the company is a place they would like to work just as much as we are assessing the applicant.

We need diversity within teams as well as across the whole organization. I am isolating gender balance here, but this applies to all factors of diversity.

Retaining and Attracting a Diverse Workforce

Many organizations are struggling with attracting and retaining a talented and diverse workforce. In our wonderful interview with Dr. Alessandra Wall on The Leadership Project podcast [22] we discovered we had these words "attract and retain" in the wrong order.

If we are to attract new diverse talent into our organizations we must first work on retaining the diverse talent that we already have.

To retain a talented and diverse workforce, we need to work on the same principles as we have discussed in this book. It becomes increasingly important when it comes to people from diverse backgrounds. People that have experienced years, decades, and generations of bias are more acutely tuned to their need to be valued, respected, and heard.

The keys to retaining and attracting a diverse and talented workforce include:

- Ensuring the vision, purpose, and impact of the organization is clear (People want to work for a company where they can see and be proud of the meaning and impact of what they do)
- Staying true to values and beliefs
- Creating a psychologically safe environment
- Making sure that every single person feels that they matter, they are valued, and their voice is being heard

With these factors in place, you will retain your existing talent and will attract new talent to join the team. New prospective talent will see an organization and team that they will see themselves being a part of. A talented and diverse team with vision, purpose, and meaning where everyone is achieving joy and fulfillment in what they do. A place where everyone feels that they belong. A place where everyone feels that they matter.

A moment of self-reflection

Take a look at your organization now. Your company, your departments, your team.

1. Do you have diversity across the organization?
2. Do you have diversity within teams and functional departments?
3. Is diversity just an arbitrary target or something that the company truly embraces?
4. Is diversity just on gender balance or does your organization take a broader view?
5. What actions can you take to influence diversity in your team and company?
6. What message are you sending to people about your culture, your purpose, vision and impact, and the environment you are creating?

Chapter Eighteen

Inclusion

What is Inclusion?

A moment that I will never forget (for good and bad reasons) is my first business trip to France as part of the Thales Group. It was not my first trip to France, but was my first within Thales. The key part that has stuck with me for many years are the memories of sitting in meetings where every time there was any heated exchange on a difficult topic that the conversation would quickly revert to French. At the time, my French was basic at best and I was immediately excluded from the conversation as I could not keep up. The observation here is not about language. I was in France, and therefore I was the visitor, and it was on me to learn both the French language and very importantly, French business customs. The observation here is purely about how I felt at this moment. It was not just in the business meeting; it also applied to social settings and discussions over lunch, dinner, and wine.

So, how did I feel at these moments? Imagine sitting in a meeting where you make a very important point (in your opinion) and you get an immediate body language reaction and a bunch of people that metaphorically huddle and talk (sometimes aggressively) in French. I did not really know if I had offended them, delighted them, provoked them in a good or bad way. In a social setting, when they would laugh among themselves, I did not know if they were laughing at me or with me and so on and so forth.

Once again, this is not about language, but rather remembering how I felt at that moment.

Far too often, inclusion becomes the forgotten cousin of Diversity & Inclusion. It is a related topic, but it is also a key subject in its own right and is often misunderstood.

When defining inclusion, I do find it helpful to think about its opposite: exclusion. Exclusion is that feeling you have when you feel you don't belong. Think back to high school and there were always the "in-crowd" and the "misfits" and students gathering in "cliques." Now remember how that felt. It is not nice when you feel that you don't belong, and no one deserves to feel that way, including in the workplace.

This will manifest itself into something I call "heavy-leg syndrome." This is the feeling you get when you arrive at work, you really don't want to be there, you look at the staircase (metaphorical or physical), and your legs start to feel physically heavy like you don't want to lift them up the stairs.

Beyond the fact that no one deserves or wants to feel that awful and deep feeling of not belonging, it is also very bad for business, productivity, and overall team performance. Someone that feels excluded is never going to operate at their full personal potential. They are also not going to feel that they can contribute to the conversation. They may have the single best idea to solve a problem or grow the business, but they just don't know how to voice it and be heard. This greatly diminishes the benefits of group thinking and brainstorming. The concept behind group thinking is that team members bounce ideas off each other, and each idea builds on the previous one. If one or more team members do not feel they can contribute, you are going to greatly reduce that group thinking effect that can be so powerful.

There are so many ways that exclusion can develop in your workplace and team environment if you are not careful.

It is a well-known saying that you should surround yourself with people that you know, like, and trust when you build your teams. This has a tendency to manifest itself into managers and leaders employing people that they have worked with in the past. While this is something that I also do from time to time, it is also something that should be controlled.

I can illustrate a number of examples here where managers have given an overemphasized preference on recruiting people from their past. This can quickly develop into a perceived clique. Whether or not you treat these people with any favoritism, people may perceive it that way. If you are not careful that perception may even be true. If you constantly defer to those people that you brought in, meet with them and have discussions at the exclusion of others, all of the other team members will see, hear, and feel that, and exclusion starts to kick in.

I am not saying to not recruit very capable people that you have worked with before, but do make sure this is balanced and go out of your way to ensure there is no favoritism. Even innocent things like private jokes that recall the past can exacerbate that feeling.

Beyond avoiding exclusion, you also need to take proactive steps to encourage inclusion. Be aware and notice if you see anyone being left out of conversations and or social interactions. Take proactive steps to subtly draw them into the conversation or activity and ensure that they understand that their opinion and participation is valued.

Furthermore, keep an eye out for exclusive behavior on behalf of others (team members, peers, leaders, etc.) and privately and carefully point this out to them. It could very well be a blind spot for them, and they will not be able to address it if it has not been brought to their attention.

Whenever you see exclusion in practice, become an ally and address it.

Including people also means making sure there is a platform where their voice can be heard and where they feel that their opinions are valued. As mentioned earlier in the book, "getting people a seat at the table is not enough." Feeling included is feeling that you belong, feeling that you are valued, and feeling that you matter.

Circling back to my own experience here. As many years passed, I developed a very rewarding career in Thales (a place I have many fond memories of). Over a period of time, I started to see similar patterns emerging. I distinctly remember taking another young Australian engineer on a business trip to France. This was his first trip there and he spoke zero French. One day on that trip, I had an almost out-of-body experience where I noticed I had fallen into the same trap. Over years working for Thales I had improved my French to an Intermediate level, enough to be conversational with many of my colleagues and team members. On this bright and cold day, I found myself engaged in conversation in French and looked over to see this young engineer with a perplexed look on his face, and I immediately saw myself from 10 years previous. At that moment, I took a proactive step to include him in the conversation. We did continue in French as appropriate, but I took the extra step of describing the conversation so he had no anxiety about what the conversation was about and felt that he could also contribute.

Once again, I must emphasize that this lesson is not at all about language, and I do not expect that people should all speak my language whenever I am around. The observation is merely about tapping into what it "feels" like when you are excluded and to always take proactive steps when you see any form of exclusion in your teams or in your workplace.

In summary:

- No one should feel that feeling of exclusion
- It is not good for their mental health and emotional wellbeing
- It is also not good for the business or team as you will be closing down the motivation, productivity, and ideation of that team member
- Be careful of unconscious exclusivity through cliques forming in your team
- Be on the lookout for any kind of exclusion and address it when you see it
- Take proactive steps to create an environment of inclusion in both professional and social circles
- Give people a platform where their voice can be heard, let them roar, and listen with an open mind, open heart, and open will.

A moment of self-reflection

I would like you to now take a moment and consider the above in your own context and teams:

1. Have you felt this feeling of exclusion before?
2. Do you believe that you may have elements of exclusion in your team or workplace?
3. Are there any cliques forming?
4. Are there perceptions of exclusion, even if unintended?
5. What proactive steps will you take to foster inclusive behavior and address any exclusion that you notice?

Chapter Nineteen

Unconscious Bias

What is unconscious bias?

Unconscious bias (sometimes referred to as implicit bias) are social stereotypes about certain groups of people that individuals form outside their own conscious awareness. Everyone does have them and an interesting phenomena is that these biases are often diametrically opposed to your own personal values and beliefs.

When you pay close attention, you will see this in everyday life.

This can be anything from unconsciously judging someone (or drawing a conclusion about someone) based on anything from their age, gender, color of their skin, gender identity, sexual preference, or physical appearance.

These assumptions can be positive or negative perceptions of the person, but in either case it is a bias that can cause problems. Examples could include that an older person is not up to speed with the latest social media technology, that a young person is not worldly enough to have clear views on the world, that a heavier set person could not be a world-class athlete (I will let Serena Williams dispel that one for you), that a well-dressed person is more successful in life than a casually dressed person, and the list goes on.

Managing Unconscious Bias

Everybody has it. There are some people that know how to identify and manage it in a better way, but everybody has it.

Even with a high focus on diversity and inclusion, unconscious bias (if left unchecked) will hold you back.

I was on a Zoom call with my leadership team recently and noticed my own unconscious bias kicking in. One positive thing about the COVID-19 pandemic, and two years (and counting) of working from home, is that we are getting a unique window into people's home life. For better and worse there has been a blurring of the boundary between work and home. On the positive, we are discovering new sides to people that we normally just see in the office or the work environment.

A great illustration of this is that we are seeing parents and how they interact with their children. Whether it be a child zooming through the room in a Spiderman outfit or just a child needing help to get a glass of water or with help connecting to home schooling.

On this day, I found myself admiring the parental skills of our marketing director, Lauren Jochum. The thought that crossed my mind was amazement at how she managed to juggle a full-time job while looking after four kids that also needed her attention.

So, where does the bias creep in? Well, I noticed that I did not have the same feeling toward my male team members, some of whom also have four kids at home.

So, I too have unconscious bias that creeps in and has most likely built up over a long period of time of observing social norms.

How and when does unconscious bias start?

On a beautiful Singapore morning, I received a life-changing message from my wife. I was playing tennis with my friends and she was patiently waiting for me to get home but couldn't contain her excitement any longer. Like so many before and after us we had the exciting news that we were pregnant.

With everything happening around us, this led to thoughts of what kind of world we were bringing a baby into. Is it a world that we are proud of? Is it a harmonious and safe world? And how do we ensure that we create an environment of opportunity? How do we ensure we pass on strong values to our children as they grow?

One thing that became increasingly apparent is that, despite some improvement, we still live in a world of prejudice. It is predominantly a "man's world" full of gender inequality, racism, and racial hate still plagues many societies, and a world full of unconscious bias.

These events now have me questioning the source or sources of this unconscious bias, including whether it starts even before we are born before being reinforced in everyday life from our early years.

As all parents would understand, my wife, Sei, and I went through the nervous and impatient game of wanting to tell the whole world of our exciting news but needing to wait until it was safe and appropriate to do so.

Once we got through that nervous period, this is where the story of unconscious bias and my questioning begins. As the weeks and months progressed, and we excitedly shared our news with family and friends that we were going to have a baby boy, we were constantly greeted with comments like "Oh Mick, you must be so proud." You could put this down to just a turn of phrase or being nice, but body language and beaming smiles would indicate a genuine feeling that I should be proud that we were having a boy. This has always begged a question for me: if I had said we were having a girl, would we have been greeted with "Oh, better luck next time" or worse "Oh, you must be so disappointed."

You can say I am being over-dramatic or exaggerating, but the sentiment that I should be somehow prouder to have a boy felt very real to me and it is just not right.

The next step in reinforcing this bias came shortly after the birth of Thomas, and it came time to name him and register his birth. While there are some people and cultures that buck this trend, for the most part, the society norm is for the child to take the father's family name. Furthermore, if the child's parents are married it is most likely that the mother has already changed their name to match their husband. There are more and more exceptions to this, with same-sex families for example, but the overwhelming majority still sticks to this tradition.

So my questions are, who decided that the man's name is more important? Does this reinforce gender bias? And is it time to change this up for good?

Things do not necessarily get any better once the new-born baby gets home. During their formative years, when they are most impressionable, children are constantly confronted with messages that reinforce gender bias. Even quite modern and recent television programs like Cocomelon have a bias within. It is clear that the producers have attempted some level of balance, but it is not quite there. The mother in the show is seen as more of a homemaker and when the father does things around the house, it is somehow depicted as "special." Furthermore, whenever there is an odd number of characters there are always more boys than girls. For example, five pandas jumping on the bed, five ducks at swimming, or even the family of three kids all have boys in the majority.

Beyond gender bias, racial bias also kicks in from a very young age. Children are born color blind to race, you can see it in their early interactions with other children in playgrounds. However, it does not take too long for children to be presented with racial bias. Even beloved books from my childhood like Dr. Seuss; when I look back now I can see clear examples of racial bias. You don't need to look very hard in social media and in everyday life to see this bias being reinforced.

You could argue that I am being over critical or that another bias, confirmation bias, is meaning that I am seeing these things because I am looking for them. However, for me these unconscious biases are very real and we must address them if we are going to make a lasting change in gender and racial equality in the world.

My personal call to action is to make sure that I am the best possible role model to Thomas and his brother Henry as they grow up. To show them there is no place in the world for bias and prejudice. It is also to be an ally to anyone who experiences bias, prejudice, or exclusion and to call it out when I see something that is just not right.

To make longer lasting and more impactful change, I do believe we need to continue to challenge societal norms. We may be past the misogynistic era of Bridgerton where a woman's value was only measured by their ability to attract the attention of suitors and a husband, but we still have a long way to go.

Far more than just a gender, age or race issue

There are many, many other biases that creep into our view. Another example stemmed from a launch video that my team and I made for Umomobility.com. In the production of the video, we made a clear and precise effort to ensure we reflected people from all walks of life. This was something very important to us and was a reflection of our values and beliefs that mobility is a human right and mobility solutions need to be accessible to all.

The video included a scene where a hospital worker was pushing a patient in a wheelchair before catching the bus home at the end of her shift.

The surprising (but well-meaning) comment we received was "Why is the underprivileged woman a woman of color?" The accusation/question inferred that we had racial bias within the video. But just pause a moment and think of what was said here.

The unconscious bias here has nothing to do with race. There was nothing in that video that indicated that the character was underprivileged. Yes, she was a hospital worker, but nothing would indicate whether she was a nurse, a doctor, a ward, or a specialist. Even if she was a nurse, I believe that every nurse I have ever met does this job due to a higher calling that they want to help people and not because they are underprivileged.

Secondly, there was an inference that if the woman was taking public transit (the bus) then she must be underprivileged. This reflects a societal stigma that public transit is only for the poor that cannot afford a car.

This is a stigma that we really must address in the world. Public transit is for everyone. I, for one, have not owned a car for more than 13 years (except for a small period), and I have a preference for taking public transit instead of owning my own car, and it is certainly not because I can't afford one.

So, unconscious bias can sneak up in all kinds of ways. For you personally, for your team, and for society as a whole. You need to keep an eye out for this and address it when you see it. Notice it in yourself and keep yourself accountable. When you see it in others, bring it to their attention (everyone has blind spots).

Unconscious Bias in the Workplace

The workplace is certainly not immune to the unconscious bias we see in society. Pantene, the shampoo company, created an award-winning commercial that highlighted examples of unconscious gender bias.

This wonderful commercial showed men and women in near identical situations and showed the labels that are applied to them.

The male dominating a meeting in his large corner office was labeled as the "boss," and the woman labeled as "bossy."

The male giving an inspirational speech was labeled as "persuasive," and the woman as "pushy."

A man working long hours was depicted as "dedicated" and the shot of the woman had carefully curated lighting creating images of a baby's cot being cast as a shadow on the wall with the word "selfish" created from the mobile above the crib.

A man that takes pride in his facial appearance is seen as "neat" and the woman as "vain."

A man dressing well is shown as "smooth" and the woman is a "show-off."

The message is extremely powerful and is underpinned by a call to action to not let "labels hold you back" and to "be strong and shine" with some not-so-subtle messaging relating to their signature products.

One thing that I must add with this point of gender bias is that both sexes are prone to this. For example, women can be equally (or even more so) guilty of having unconscious bias or even judgment of other women. All of the labels mentioned in the Pantene commercial I have heard women use when discussing their counterparts. Furthermore, working mothers will often "feel" this judgment even if it is not stated.

With the shoe on the other foot, most of us also have unconscious bias related to men with assumptions that we will not be as good at "soft skills," that we will not be able to change nappies (diapers), or cannot find things in the cupboard that are staring us right in the face (oh, hang on, that last one is true—at least for me it is).

Back to a more serious note, men will feel judged in the workplace if they leave early one day to see their children's concert performance at school. Just as women will feel judgment or guilt for missing that school event, the men will feel they are being judged for not being dedicated at work and for putting his family first.

In summary, there is no place for any of this bias, prejudice, or guilt, and we must work together to see an end to it.

Within your team, one positive action you can take is to collectively empower everyone to call out unconscious bias when it creeps in. Everyone has blind spots. The blind spots cannot be addressed unless they are brought into the light.

A moment of self-reflection

This may be a challenging one. For the next two weeks, I challenge you to look around you.

1. What unconscious bias (of all types) do you see?
2. Do you see the unconscious bias of others?
3. Do you recognize your own?
4. What are the biases in your team?
5. What are the biases in your company?
6. What action will you take to address it? To notice it, name it, and not let it influence your leadership and decision making?

Chapter Twenty

Priority Management

If *everything* is your highest priority, then everything is also your lowest priority.

In workplaces all over the world this is a common issue. Staff are looking to their leadership for guidance on priorities and how to best use their time. We are all given 24 hours every day, and we need to make effective use of that constrained resource.

In some cases, staff look to their leader for some kind of signal or direction and receive mixed messages about what is important. In other cases, it is far worse with leaders giving explicit statements like "everything is the highest priority" or giving contradictory statements from one day to the next.

When giving guidance to staff on conflicting priorities it represents a great learning and coaching opportunity. Try starting with asking them what they think is the highest priority. You will be surprised how often they know the answer themselves and they are just looking for confirmation.

A great story I once heard came from Liz Wiseman, author of *Multipliers* [3]. Liz's amazing book describes the differences in leadership style between "Multipliers" and "Diminishers."

One of the experiments in the book is called *Extreme Questions*. In this concept the idea is to conduct an entire meeting where all you do is ask questions and see how your team thinks and reacts.

In the story shared by Liz, she speaks of a working parent (in this case a mother) who has had a very long and exhausting day at work. As she approaches home and readies herself for the nightly battle of the evening kids' ritual she decides to try the Extreme Questions experiment at home. Instead of telling her kids what to do, she asked, "What's first?"

"Homework."

"What's next?"

"Dinner."

"Then?"

"Bath," they would reply, and so on and so forth.

The moral to the story is that people often do know exactly what they need to do, they just need to be given the right environment to think and be independent.

Ask yourself before you give direction to your team; is it the same with them? Will they grow more if you ask rather than tell?

Explain why

In the event that your team does not manage to self-explore and determine their own priorities, you may need to guide them. If you do need to do this, take the time to explain why X is a higher priority to Y. That way there is a higher probability that next time they will self-determine their own priorities and they will do so with increased accuracy, efficiency, and confidence.

Opportunity Cost

Another key concept that all leaders need to have a solid grasp of is opportunity cost. The fundamental principle of opportunity cost is by choosing to say yes to one thing, you are also saying no to something else.

This could be financial with regard to where you apply budget and employ capital, it could be the application of scarce resources, or it could be the allocation of your own time or the time of your team.

It is important to ask yourself these questions from time to time:

1. By saying yes to this, what am I saying no to?
2. What am I not doing right because of the things I am doing?
3. Are those things more or less important or urgent than these things?

Opportunity qualification

The concept of opportunity qualification is directly applicable to anyone leading a sales organization but also be applied more broadly.

The concepts here are the same. You have finite resources, including time and budget, and you need to ensure you are making smart decisions.

When I took on my very first executive role, I found that my sales team was trying to chase, bid, and win no fewer than 36 large opportunities at once. I quickly drew the conclusion that if we followed that path we would win exactly zero of those contracts. So, I made the tough decision that we would need to drastically cut that. Rather than submit 36 poor tenders, I decided that we would focus on just five and put our hearts and souls into them.

History has shown that we went on to win three of those five, putting a large chunk of profitable work in the backlog. I'm not sure about you, but I would pick winning three out of five over winning 0/36 any day of the week

How did we determine which five?

We broke this down to three simple questions:

1. Is it real?

This question relates to the commitment of the customer and the certainty the project will proceed. This includes assessing if they have a budget.

There is nothing worse than winning a tender or competition only to have the project be canceled

2. Can we win?

There are multi-facets to this question. They include:

Does the customer know, like, and trust us? Do we have more customer intimacy than others? Do they have an edge on us?

Do we have the right solution to meet their needs?

Who are the competitors?

3. Is it worth winning?

There are some cases where we could win but it wouldn't be worth it. For example, the margin is too low or the risk is too high, or it could be that we can win this one project and there are no follow-up projects behind it. Whereas another opportunity may be smaller, but with many more opportunities and a market that opens up from that initial project.

In following this process, have your team articulate what they believe is important and why. They will create a virtuous learning cycle and your collective decision making will improve over time.

Prioritizing your own time

When managing your own time as a leader, you need to always consider the question of force multiplication. Force multiplication is about the ability to expand your own personal reach and impact through collaboration with others. Always remember that you are only one person. You are given 24 hours per day just like everyone else. No matter how productive you are personally, there will always be the limitation of hours in the day. No one can change that. What you can do is unlock the productivity in others. A key question is to consider is whether any of your team members are waiting on something from you. While waiting, are they blocked from proceeding further with their work. In terms of prioritizing your own work, you may wish to see if any of the tasks in your to-do list will take a small amount of your time but will unblock the work of one or more of your team members and hence be a force multiplication.

Decision Fatigue and Outsourcing

Other key techniques to help manage your own time and energy include making sure you do indeed delegate, avoiding decision fatigue, and outsourcing.

As a leader you need to build self-awareness of your own superpowers (what you do best) and what is the best use of your own capacity and time.

There are times you will just need to be comfortable with letting go and allowing someone else the opportunity to help you with things. If you are a small-business person or entrepreneur, this may include outsourcing to an agency or using services like Upwork and Fiverr to get things done.

Something not to be underestimated is the concept of *decision fatigue*. It can be quite exhausting to be making decisions all day every day. To maintain your energy, flow, and effectiveness, you want to ensure that the decisions you are making are the most impactful and important ones. To explore the concept of managing your decision fatigue you look to minimize smaller, less-impactful decisions through either outsourcing or removing variables. Removing or reducing variables is about limiting the options you need to consider for decisions that are really not that critical. The first level of this is to make sure there are no more than two to four options to choose from. Beyond that you will go into analysis paralysis and not make a decision. For very low-level decisions, remove all variables and just leave yourself with one choice.

This is why we see people like Steve Jobs and Mark Zuckerberg wearing the same shirt every day (for the avoidance of doubt they have multiple copies of the same shirt) as this becomes one less decision that they need to make. You could look at all of the small decisions you make in a day and see which of these would make your life simpler if that decision was removed from your daily decision-making load.

An experiment my wife and I are conducting at this very moment is alternate decision days. We are taking turns at making all of the minor daily decisions of the family. This includes deciding on what we are going to have for breakfast, lunch, and dinner, and whether we are going to take a walk or a bike ride today. So far the results are amazing. We have not just reduced decision fatigue, it has also given us time back in our day. Previously, a decision around meal time would inevitably go something like this:

"What do you want for dinner tonight?"

"I don't know; what would you like?"

"I don't know; it's up to you."

"No, it's up to you."

"I am happy with anything."

Etc, etc…

This has now been replaced with the alternate decisions, and on my day, it would go something like this: "We are having Japanese for dinner."

And my wife would say, "Great."

Then we get on with ourselves and enjoy our meal together without any stress.

Take some time to think about daily decisions you make in your life (home and work). What are the decisions you could outsource or reduce the variables? The more you reduce the total number of decisions you make the more you will be able to focus and make well-thought-out decisions for the important stuff.

Avoid Multitasking, try time blocking

A team at the University of Michigan [23] has now proven that humans cannot multitask, our brains can only do one thing at a time. However, what we can be capable of is fast task switching. There is no doubt that some people are better at fast task switching than others. However, studies are repeatedly showing that people (including leaders) are far more productive when they just don't do it.

Instead of trying multitasking, experiment with time blocking. Time blocking is where you dedicate blocks of time to a single task with no distractions. A very present example is writing this book. This book would never get written if I did not set aside blocks of time where writing is my sole focus. There are multiple ways of doing this. Many people find that 45–90 minutes is a great window to use.

The secret is to balance between start, stop, and transfer times. If an activity takes 15–20 minutes to restart, to remember where you were, and get productive again, then you need to allocate much more than 20 minutes to that task to make any meaningful progress.

Consider your calendar for the next week. Are you just jumping from one task (or meeting) to another? Could you achieve much more if you time block and focus your energies on one thing at a time for a greater length of time? For most people the answer is yes.

Another thing I have experimented with during the writing of this book has been binaural beats. I have been using an app called Brain.fm that uses different binaural beats and sounds for different functional activities. It has modes for deep sleep and as well as modes for immersive work. When writing this book, I have been creating 90-minute blocks of time and use Brain.fm's modes for Deep Work or Creative Flow depending on what stage of book production I was at. I have been super impressed with the results and highly recommend that you give it a try and see if it is suitable for you.

7 Mindful Questions

A great reference that I would highly recommend when considering personal and team prioritisation is 7 Mindful Questions by Lisa Nezneski [24]. The book is about the practice of mindfulness and is centred around 7 questions that I find very valuable in thinking about how I spend my time. Next time you are pondering whether you and your team are using your time effectively, please do consider these questions:

1. What am I doing right now?
2. Why am doing this?
3. Why is that important?
4. What else should (or could) I be doing?
5. What is essential?
6. What could I do better? And
7. What is the best choice right now?

Effective Delegation

Delegation is an essential skill in any leader's toolkit. Among many reasons, there is no way that you can develop a high-performance team if you try to do everything. Firstly, there are only so many hours in the day, you may not be the most skilled person in your team for that task, and it is a missed opportunity for engagement and learning among your team members.

So, if delegation is important, how do you do it effectively?

There is no one single answer to that question. Every single person has a different preferred working style when it comes to delegation and even the same person may have different needs depending on their level of skill and experience with the topic at hand.

My strong preference is to err toward providing as much clarity as possible on the purpose (why) of the task or the problem that is trying to be solved and less on telling specifics of how it should be done.

This generates empowerment and ownership on behalf of the individuals and fosters their creativity in coming up with innovative solutions.

The other things to be clear would be:

1. The deadline you expect them to meet
2. Any stakeholders that need to be engaged
3. To provide an open door and psychologically safe environment for them to come back to you if they need help throughout the project or task

There are exceptions where you may indeed have someone that needs more guidance on the how, and the what, but the clear preference is to focus your clarity on the why and the when.

A great experiment that illustrates this perfectly is a team building game called remote chess, which is both an exercise of communication and delegation. The game is set up with two team leaders being separated from their teams with only mobile phones or handheld radios for communication. The leaders are asked to remotely direct their team based on the report sent back to them. The team in the field typically report back that they are standing in front of a chess board and the leaders are given the mission to "win the game."

Almost invariably, most leaders then start drawing a chess board on a piece of paper and start navigating and telling the team every move to make on the chess board.

However, the simplest path in this exercise is to simply ask questions to their team:

1. Do you or anyone on the team know how to play chess?
2. Who is our best chess player?
3. Okay, your mission is to "win the game." Call me when you are done.

This is a perfect illustration of empowerment, engagement, and trust while delegating. The secret to this game/exercise is not to try to win the game of chess remotely or thinking through every move yourself. The secret is to identify who is your best chess player and empower them to get on with it.

Balancing Decisiveness with Empowerment and Inclusion

While I have a strong preference toward empowerment, engagement, buy-in, and inclusion, there are some times when leaders are looked upon for decisiveness.

These times include a time of crisis. History has shown many strong leaders that are able to be decisive at moments of great need. To be clear, being decisive does not mean not listening or not making informed decisions, but it can mean acting swiftly based on the best information available at that time.

Decisiveness is also important when it comes to matters relating to the core values and culture of the team. When behaviors are out of line with the values of the team, it is important to be true to those values and be decisive and clear in response.

With the above in mind, I give my team license to directly ask for decisiveness when they need it. I am very open that my style is more of a coaching approach with empowerment and engagement. Therefore, when they come to me with questions, they know that my natural tendencies will lead me to asking them some open questions to help them discover their own answer. However, if there is a good reason why they just need an answer on a particular occasion, they are also empowered to be upfront with me and say that they just need a rapid answer on this one. I encourage you to do the same. Your team will appreciate this.

Running Effective Meetings

A common complaint of staff in many organizations is the conduct of inefficient or ineffective meetings. This has been further exacerbated in recent times with COVID-19 driving us to a predominantly work-from-home environment. People are finding themselves jumping from Zoom meeting to Zoom meeting, and at the end of the day they have Zoom fatigue and can't honestly say what they achieved that day.

As a leader, you are going to find yourself faced with the need to facilitate meetings and an expectation from your team that these meetings be efficient and effective.

Many people will say that the key to a great meeting is to have a pre-set agenda. I personally refine that a little further and would say the key is to have a declared purpose and desired outcome of the meeting.

"The purpose of this meeting is to _____. The outcome we are seeking is _____. This is important because _____."

Create and share these statements when sending out the meeting invite and repeat them again at the start of the meeting to get everyone in the right mindset and frame.

Some other considerations for running effective meetings are as follows:

1. Decide if the meeting is necessary at all. Consider if the purpose and outcome can be effectively achieved in another way
2. Invite only those people that genuinely need to be there (but no fewer). Each person should have a personal reason for being there, even if that reason is personal growth
3. Make the meeting as short as possible (but no shorter) to achieve the outcome

4. If it will streamline the process, provide a read-ahead in the days leading up to the meeting (and expect people to read it)

5. Open the meeting with a short reminder on the purpose and desired outcome

6. Close the meeting with a succinct summary of what just happened (any decisions made, clarity on next steps, actions, and accountabilities)

Depending on the purpose of the meeting, you should also consider talking less and listening more. As stated before, a great leader knows when to be the first to speak versus when to be the last. If the purpose of the meeting is communicating an update then you may end up doing more speaking, but if the purpose is to seek solutions and a diverse set of ideas, you should provide space and a psychologically safe environment for everyone to have their say.

A key reflection of some of the most inspiring leaders I have had has been the ability to listen and succinctly summarize. Chris Jenkins, CEO and Chairman of Thales Australia, had a remarkable ability to quietly listen to, and observe, his entire executive team debate a topic in detail. As the meeting would draw to conclusion, he was able to summarize in one to three short statements what needed to be done. Invariably, the team members, who have all just been debating, would all look at each other with a knowing look of "Hey, he's right…again." Not right just because he was the boss, but right because he had that uncanny ability to sift, sort, and prioritize what was material and was immaterial to the current topic. This is something I will always admire and strive to be able to do.

This is a skill that you may need to develop over time and consciously practice. It can be very difficult to say nothing when you watch your team debating. It becomes even more difficult if the subject is something where you have deep expertise. But remember, this environment fosters diversity of thought and provides wonderful growth opportunities for your team and all of the team members.

You may even find yourself in meetings where you have discovered the answer to the problem in the first 10 minutes, particularly if you have a sharp mind, but if you blurt out the answer at that moment you will miss the wonderful opportunity to watch your team find the answer and blossom. Furthermore, if they find the answer themselves, they will take 1,000 percent more ownership and buy-in to the solution, and you will all be better for the experience.

You do not need to be the smartest person in the room, and you certainly do not need to *prove* you are the smartest in the room.

Once you perfect this (and I am still trying), something very surprising will come. You will get far more personal satisfaction from watching your team grow than just being respected for your own abilities. There is something deep and emotional that happens inside me when my team members develop and they self-discover answers without my intervention.

This may also take time for your team to get used to as well. Particularly if they are used to a more directive style. If this is the case, and you are concerned that the silence will be responded with more silence, consider pre-preparing a set of open-ended questions that will promote discussion instead of jumping to the answer. Examples could include:

- What do you think is the real challenge here?
- What would success look like?
- What would need to be true to achieve that?
- What barriers to success do you see?
- How can we overcome those barriers?

Moment of **self-reflection**

Take a moment now to stop, think, and reflect. Reflect on:

1. Great and inspiring leaders you have had in the past and consider how they prioritized, how they ran meetings, and their communication style
2. Poor managers you have had—what they did and how they made you feel
3. Poor meetings you had had—how were they run?
4. Your own style—what is working well? What is not working? What will you change in the future?

Chapter Twenty-One

Feedback is a Gift

This is a challenging topic for me to write about. I will openly admit that this has not traditionally been an area of strength for me. However, I do have plenty of lessons learned to share with you and can share my experiences of how I overcome challenges here.

For many years I had an aversion to having challenging conversations with staff members, peers, and my bosses. If I am brutally honest, I would say it has also impacted my personal life at different times.

This issue has, in the past, manifested itself into anxiety about providing negative or constructive feedback to others. Leading up to a discussion that I know that I "have to have," I would inevitably procrastinate and put it off as long as I possibly could. This would result in anguish and mental stress on my part as it would eat away at me the whole time.

It is not completely clear to me where this anxiety comes from. I feel it is a mixture of things. I dedicate my life, my personal why, to making people's lives less stressful. For example, The Leadership Project movement was started with a drive to make people's work lives happier and less stressful through better leadership at all levels in organizations. Bringing humanistic and emotionally intelligent values back into the world of leadership. So, at least in part, the anxiety was related to a fear of making people unhappy and more stressed. Beyond that, there was the element of just avoiding confrontation. Most people do not like confrontation, but for me, this seemed even more so. I am not going to delve into any deep or dark secret in my upbringing that made this the case. I can't pick any one event that would have led to that and it would not be helpful to the story anyway. The other aspect is a hint of "what will they think of me?" Or "will they hate me?" And potentially an over-zealous need to be liked.

To make matters worse, what would typically happen is the longer I would put off that challenging conversation, the worse the performance issue or situation would get. A delayed conversation would typically end up being even more challenging than if I had addressed the situation earlier.

The interesting thing is that I had clear self-awareness about the issue, and I knew the whole time that this anxiety was not rational, but this doesn't make the emotion any less real for me. Delaying typically leads to a lot of protracted angst, unnecessary workload and rework to be done, and once the situation is addressed, the response is typically "Oh, you should have told me sooner and I could have done something about it."

I knew this was all irrational for multiple reasons. Firstly, in my entire (and long) career, I had only ever had these conversations go badly on three occasions—two that were related to termination discussions, and one where the other party did not have self-awareness that their behavior (a form of bullying) was unacceptable.

The second reason this anxiety was irrational was that I personally thrive on feedback. I enjoy feedback, both positive and constructive, and have actively sought it out at appropriate moments throughout my career. Feedback has enabled me to build on my strengths and helped me to identify blind spots in my own personal performance that I needed to address to become a better leader. I am often heard to say "If I don't know about it (awareness), I cannot fix it or do something about it." It took me a long time, too long, to realize that the vast majority of people feel the same. Others also thrive on feedback. Positive feedback to lift them up (something that I was already good at) and constructive feedback to help them identify their weaknesses so they can address them and improve their performance. For me, this has applied universally with staff members, peers, and bosses. All have welcomed feedback gleefully and generally thanked me for it (with the above three exceptions mentioned earlier). I have even had opportunities to give senior executives in customer organizations some tactfully delivered feedback that they graciously accepted. The common theme is that without awareness they cannot address the issue and (most) are thankful that someone has brought it to their attention.

Providing that feedback has usually led to higher levels of respect and certainly no aspect of being less liked.

So, the lessons I have personally taken from the above experience include:

1. Feedback is a gift
2. I thrive on feedback and so do most others
3. Without awareness, people cannot address their shortcomings
4. Giving feedback is act of love
5. Giving feedback increases the recipient's level of respect for you

Moment of self-reflection

Take a moment now to stop, think, and reflect:

1. Do you like to receive feedback?
2. How do you like to receive feedback?
3. Does your team also enjoy receiving feedback?
4. What are their preferences for receiving feedback?
5. Does your approach match these preferences?

Chapter Twenty-Two

Conclusion

I do hope that you have enjoyed this book and found it to be useful in your journey to becoming a high-performance leader. Leadership is indeed a journey. It is a journey of self-discovery, a journey of discovering the human psyche, and a journey paved with continuous learning opportunities.

Don't forget to take advantage of the downloadable Leadership Journal that accompanies this book. This will help you greatly to put the practice of self-reflection into place as you continue your learning as a leader.

Always take the time to look around and learn from other leaders. What are they doing that is working well? What are they doing that is *not* working well? What can you learn from that?

Learn from your own successes and failures every day as you strive to be a better leader.

Take the time to consider why you want to be a leader and to be clear about your purpose, impact, values, and beliefs.

Continually practice emotional intelligence and always remember that leadership is not about you.

We look forward to bringing more great thought-provoking content and learnings in future books in this series.

In the meantime, please do take care, look out for each other, and always remember to challenge the status quo.

Moment of self-reflection

As we draw to a conclusion of this book, I would like you to take the time to stop, think, and reflect on what you have taken away from this book with the following questions:

1. What has been your greatest learning from what you have read?
2. Are there any emerging properties from putting all of the learnings together collectively?
3. How will you put these learnings into practice?
4. How will it enable a continuous learning cycle?
5. Will you help others to also find their way in the world of leadership?

More from The Leadership Project

We would love to hear from you and see you get involved in The Leadership Project movement. We have built a strong community of like-minded people that want to see change in the world of leadership. We practice the principles detailed in this book to create a psychologically safe environment for people to discuss and work on their leadership craft. We embrace key principles of how people prefer to learn including collaborative (or social) learning, micro learning, gamification, coaching, and mentoring.

You can find out more about The Leadership Project and all of our forums, webinars, courses, training, service, and materials at the following links:

Download The Leadership Project Self-Reflection Journal (a wonderful complement to this very book) at

https://www.mickspiers.com/yourealeadernowwhat . The Leadership Project Self-Reflection Journal will help you implement the lessons shared in this book.

Review The Leadership Project courses, training, and services at

www.mickspiers.com

Join The Leadership Project Facebook Community Group at

https://www.facebook.com/groups/334571975014326

Subscribe to our YouTube channel full of useful videos at

https://www.youtube.com/channel/UCPG9X7weoI4Xs3SreZab1rQ

Follow us on LinkedIn at https://www.linkedin.com/company/the-leadership-proj/

Bibliography

1. Gallup. (2021). (rep.). State of the Global Workplace.

2. Spiers. M. Podcast – Lead with Purpose and Meaning – Zach Mercurio. The Leadership Project. (2021). Retrieved April 16, 2022, from https://www.mickspiers.com/podcast/episode/4fcd6d1e/031-lead-with-purpose-and-meaning-zach-mercurio

3. Wiseman, L., McKeown, G., & Covey, S. R. (2017). Multipliers: How the best leaders make everyone smarter. Harper Business.

4. Gostick, A. R., & Elton, C. (2012). All in: How the best managers create a culture of belief and drive big results. Free Press.

5. Glasser, W. (2001). Choice theory: A new psychology of personal freedom. HarperPerennial.

6. Glasser, W. (2001). Choice theory in the classroom. Quill.

7. Sharma , Akshanka. (2016). Designing Learning for millennials. ATD.

8. National Geographic . (2018). Brain Games Conformity Waiting Room - YouTube. Brain Games Conformity Waiting Room. Retrieved April 16, 2022, from https://www.youtube.com/watch?v=X6kWygqR0L8

9. Asch, S. E. (1956). Studies of independence and conformity: I. A minority of one against a unanimous majority. Psychological monographs: General and applied, 70(9), 1-70

10. Spiers, M. (2021). Podcast - How to Measure Culture – Sulin Lau. The Leadership Project. Retrieved April 16, 2022, from https://www.mickspiers.com/podcast/episode/4b54fe65/episode-04-sulin-lau-of-grab-part-1

11. Spiers, M. (2021). Podcast - Agile Transformation – Anne Parmer. The Leadership Project. Retrieved April 16, 2022, from https://www.mickspiers.com/podcast/episode/4d6db9ab/episode-11-agile-transformation-with-anne-parmer

12. Sinek, S. (2010). Start with why: How great leaders inspire everyone to take action. Penguin Audio.

13. Mercurio, Z. (2017). The invisible leader: Transform your life, work, and organization with the power of authentic purpose. Advantage.

14. Seligman, M. (2017). Authentic happiness: Using the new positive psychology to realise your potential for lasting fulfillment. Nicholas Brealey Publishing.

15. Spiers, M. (2021). Podcast - Finding Purpose and Impact – Kimberley Abbott. The Leadership Project. Retrieved April 16, 2022, from https://www.mickspiers.com/podcast/episode/4989a802/episode-23-finding-purpose-and-impact-kimberley-abbott-part-1

16. Spiers, M. (2021). Podcast - Your Personality and Uniqueness – Gary Williams. The Leadership Project. Retrieved April 16, 2022, from https://www.mickspiers.com/podcast/episode/4a8be24e/032-your-personality-and-uniqueness-with-gary-williams

17. Goleman, D. (1995). Emotional intelligence. Toronto.

18. Scharmer, C. O. (2009). Theory U: Leading from the futures as it emerges. Berrett-Koehler Publishers, Inc.

19. Covey, S. R., Collins, J. C., & Covey, S. (2020). The 7 Habits of Highly Effective People: Powerful Lessons in Personal Change. Simon & Schuster.

20. Campbell, Don (2021). Creativity: It's Not What You Think: An Artist's Journey from Mind to Heart to the Source of All Creativity

21. Drexler, A., Sibbet, D., & Forrester, R. (1993). Team performance model: Abstract. The Grove Consultants International.

22. Spiers, M. (2021). Podcast - Attracting and Retaining Women - Dr Alessandra Wall. The Leadership Project. Retrieved April 16, 2022, from https://www.mickspiers.com/podcast/episode/4a84f1cf/episode-27-attracting-and-retain-women-in-your-organisation-dr-alessandra-wall-part-1

23. Srna, S., Schrift, R. Y., & Zauberman, G. (2018). The illusion of multitasking and its positive effect on performance. Psychological Science, 29(12), 1942–1955. https://doi.org/10.1177/095679/618801013

24. Nezneski, Lisa (2021). 7 Mindful Questions.

Leave a review at Amazon

We would love to hear what you think of this book and whether it has been useful to you. It would be greatly appreciated if you could leave an honest rating and review on Amazon. This helps other people, just like yourself, to find this book and put it to good use.

Can You Help?

Thank You For Reading My Book!

I really appreciate all of your feedback, and I love hearing what you have to say.

I need your input to make the next version of this book and my future books better.

Please leave me an honest review on Amazon letting me know what you thought of the book.

Thanks so much!

Mick

About the Author

Mick Spiers is the founder of The Leadership Project movement. He started The Leadership Project with a vision to inspire all leaders to challenge the status quo and a mission to empower modern leaders through knowledge and emotional intelligence. He has the view that leadership practices have not kept pace with an ever-changing modern world. The world is facing a leadership crisis with decreasing levels of employee engagement and increasing levels of workplace stress. People are spending up to 1/3 of their lives in workplaces they are not enjoying, and Mick is dedicating the rest of his life to help address that.

He is passionate about equity, equality, diversity, and inclusion and providing a world where everyone is treated with respect and dignity. Where their opinions are valued and they are treated like they matter. He believes that every person on the planet has their own unique superpower, and it is the role of the leader to help them find that and provide them with the environment in which they can create meaningful impact.

Mick is the host of the very successful podcast, The Leadership Project, where he feels blessed to be able to interview and learn from exceptional leaders from all walks of life.

Mick is an experienced executive with an exceptional track record of developing high-performance teams. He has had great success in every venture throughout his career. However, this has not been without many lessons learned along the way. Mick has paid close attention and has been a student of leadership throughout. He has been blessed to work under some truly inspirational leaders and also had his fair share of bad bosses along the way. Importantly, he has learned lessons from both ends of the scale. He has also studied closely his own leadership style to see what works and does not work. He practices self-reflection every day, as taught in this book, to help him improve his leadership craft continually.

Mick is a lifelong learner and continues to study psychology and key topics such as emotional intelligence to cultivate the leader he has become as he continues to grow.

Mick takes great pride in sharing these lessons with others and developing other leaders through coaching and a learning mindset.

Printed in Great Britain
by Amazon

81681185R00132